HIDEKI MATSUI

SPORTSMANSHIP, MODESTY,
AND THE ART OF THE HOME RUN

HIDEKI MATSUI

SPORTSMANSHIP, MODESTY, AND THE ART OF THE HOME RUN

·

SHIZUKA IJUIN

BALLANTINE BOOKS

NEW YORK

Copyright © 2007 by Shizuka Ijuin

Published in the United States by Ballantine Books,
an imprint of The Random House Publishing Group,
a division of Random House, Inc., New York.

BALLANTINE and colophon are registered trademarks
of Random House, Inc.

Translated by Allison Markin Powell
Adapted by Paul Witcover

Photos on pp. 1–9 used with permission of Hideki Matsui Baseball Museum, Japan;
photos on pp. 10–16 used with permission of Kyodo News Services.

Published in Japan as *Matsui Hideki no Tamashii* by Random House Kodansha.

ISBN 978-0-345-49569-3

Library of Congress Cataloging-in-Publication Data

Ijuin, Shizuka.
Hideki Matsui : sportsmanship, modesty and the art of the home run / by Shizuka Ijuin.
p. cm.
ISBN-13: 978-0-345-49569-3 (hardcover : alk. paper)
ISBN-10: 0-345-49569-1 (hardcover : alk. paper)
1. Matsui, Hideki. 2. Baseball players—Japan—Biography.
3. New York Yankees (Baseball team)—History. I. Title.
GV865.M495I65 2007
796.357092—dc22   2006102129
[B]

Printed in the United States of America

www.ballantinebooks.com

2 4 6 8 9 7 5 3 1

First Edition

Book design by Jo Anne Metsch

CONTENTS

HIDEKI MATSUI

SPORTSMANSHIP, MODESTY,
AND THE ART OF THE HOME RUN

A CHILD OF BASEBALL

April 8, 2003. I don't think I will ever forget that day.

"What a gorgeous morning," said my wife, Hiroko, as she stood on tiptoes, holding open the curtain of the window that looked out on the garden to the east of our house in Sendai, the beautiful City of Trees. Glancing up from the chair where I was sipping fragrant Chinese tea while reviewing the manuscript of my latest novel, I saw that it was indeed a beautiful spring day. The snow clouds that until yesterday had hung low over the landscape were starting to break up, and the sun was peeking through.

"It's been so long since we've seen blue sky," Hiroko continued, excitement in her voice. "I have a feeling that it's a good omen. You wait and see. Today will be a day to remember."

I knew better than to contradict my wife on such matters. Besides, I was hoping that her prediction would come true. "Just remember not to touch the television in the living room," I cautioned her. "It's all set up, okay?"

Several days earlier, an electrician had installed a new tuner that enabled us to receive more television channels than ever before. In most families, there are one or two young people who are technically savvy, but our house consisted of only a bungling writer in his late fifties, a former actress who had little experience with homemaking, and a hard-to-please dog who had the face, and often the temperament, of a dour philosopher. Between the three of us, it would be hard to say who was the least competent when it came to electronics. Ever since the new tuner had been installed, Hiroko and I had been afraid to do anything more complicated than turn the TV on and off. The reason for all of this caution was simple: Our television was set to receive live coverage of the New York Yankees' home opener against the Minnesota Twins, almost seven thousand miles away from our home in Japan. If anything went wrong with the new tuner or the TV, we would miss the major-league debut of Hideki Matsui, a moment that we had waited seven long months to see. It was a moment that Hideki, whom my wife and I had grown close to over the course of his extraordinary career in Japan, had been waiting for his entire life.

In fact, the game had been scheduled for yesterday, but there had been heavy snow in New York, and it had been called off at the last minute. Hiroko and I had been sitting expectantly in front of the television at three o'clock in the morning—the fourteen-hour difference between New York and Japan made watching the game in real time an exercise in sleep deprivation—when the announcer had broken the bad news. Now, thanks to the inscrutable ways of the baseball gods, we had almost an entire day to get through before the postponed game was played, and my wife and I were jittery with anxiety and suspense . . . and a lack of sleep. I couldn't concentrate on my novel. Hiroko busied herself about the house to no purpose that I could see. Even our dog, Ice, had picked up on the mood, wandering between us with a quizzical, slightly pained expression on his face that seemed to indicate he was pondering questions of profound philosophical significance.

"MAYBE you should go to church," I suggested to Hiroko after a while.

"Why? I just went to Sunday worship yesterday."

"You could pray for Matsui."

"I already prayed for him yesterday."

"But that was for the snowed-out game," I said. "Those prayers might not count anymore. Just to be on the safe side, I think you should pray again. You know, sort of to remind God."

My wife gave me a look I knew well. It said, "What kind of idiot did I marry?"

I would have prayed for Matsui myself, but there wasn't any reason for me to think that God would listen to my prayers, much less grant them. I had been raised in a home without religion, then had led a life of debauchery until the age of thirty, at which point I had become a writer. And deep down inside, despite my wife's influence and example, I knew that I hadn't really improved too much in all the years since. No, I would leave the praying to Hiroko, a devout Catholic.

"It's disrespectful to 'remind' God," she informed me. "Anyway, I prayed very hard that Matsui would have a good game. Everything will be all right, you'll see. Try not to worry so much."

HOURS later, I was wondering if Matsui was in need of her advice. There he was in Yankee Stadium, his cap held to his chest, a tense expression on his face as he listened to "The Star-Spangled Banner" performed by the United States Military Academy at West Point Glee Club.

"He looks a little nervous," Hiroko said, sounding more than a little nervous herself.

"Well, of course. He's standing in the ballpark of his dreams for the first time, the famous 'House that Ruth Built,'" I replied. Over the years, my wife and I had come to consider Matsui more than just a friend. This gifted young man had won a special place in our hearts. And now, watching him, I felt my heart swell with pride. The past year had been filled with difficult choices for Matsui, but he had faced them with dignity and bravery. Now, after everything, there he was, standing tall and proud in Yankee pinstripes. *Look how far you've come,* I said silently, as if he could hear my thoughts all those miles away.

As the names of the starting lineup were announced and Matsui trotted out to his position in left field, loud cheers and applause rose up from the stands. The Yankee fans were doing everything they could to make this young man from Japan feel welcome in his first home game. I knew that some fans had come all the way from Japan to see their hero play, and there were many Japanese-Americans in the stands as well. Yet despite the outpouring of support, Matsui looked a bit tentative to me as he ran to the outfield. He seemed to be reassuring himself that the grass beneath his feet was real. Or perhaps he wasn't used to the cold. According to the announcers, the temperature was a frigid thirty-five degrees.

Facing the veteran pitcher Joe Mays, Matsui's first at bat was a ground ball to second base, and though he ran hard, he was thrown out at first. He got on base his second at bat, but only by a walk. I had a feeling that the fans were beginning to wonder if Matsui could really hit major-league pitchers after all. Was his reputation as a slugger, the hitting power that had earned him the nickname "Godzilla," nothing but hype? Hiroko and I exchanged worried glances. I thought about bringing up the subject of prayers again but decided that would not be wise.

Going into the bottom of the fifth inning, the Yankees had a 3–1 lead. With one out and players on second and third base, Bernie Williams came up to bat. The Twins' catcher, A. J. Pier-zynski, stood up.

I couldn't believe my eyes. "What, an intentional walk?!" I shouted incredulously at the television.

"What's an intentional walk?" Hiroko asked. Though she followed Matsui's on-field exploits faithfully and was a big fan of his team, the Yomiuri (Tokyo) Giants (because the team is based in Tokyo, it is popularly known as the Tokyo Giants), my wife knew next to nothing about the game of baseball beyond the fact that the team with the most points at the end of nine innings was the winner. Oh yes, and that when a player hit a home run, he could make his way around the bases at a leisurely trot. She enjoyed watching that part.

"What's an intentional walk?" she asked again. "What does it mean?"

The fans in Yankee Stadium were going crazy.

I knew exactly what they were feeling. Standing in the on-deck circle was Hideki Matsui. Without looking away from the screen, I explained to my wife, "The Twins think they have a better chance of facing off against Matsui in this situation than they do against Bernie Williams."

"But by walking Williams, they're loading the bases!"

"Yes. But they think they can get Matsui out more easily than Williams. Maybe even get him to hit into a double play. It's a common tactic."

Hiroko had a hard time accepting my explanation. She seemed to take the intentional walk as some kind of affront, a personal insult directed against Matsui. "This sort of thing never happened to him in Japan, did it?"

"No, and perhaps they'll find out why."

The television showed a close-up of Matsui. He wore a determined expression, one I had seen many times before. He had been playing baseball ever since he was a boy, and it occurred to me that it had probably been many years since he'd had the experience of the batter before him being intentionally walked. Possibly not since 1993, his rookie year with the Giants, the most successful team in Japan.

But this wasn't Japan anymore. This was major-league baseball.

As I watched Mays and Pierzynski playing catch, and then Williams jogging to first base to load the bases, I reflected on the vicissitudes of life. Every person faces trials and tribulations. Even though the people around you try their best to protect you, there are inevitably situations that you must overcome on your own. And that's as it should be. Life is all about triumphing over adversity. In fact, whether you triumph or not isn't as important as facing your challenges squarely and doing the best you can. I knew this very well from my own life. Nevertheless, at that moment I resented the baseball gods a little for presenting Matsui with such a difficult test right, so to speak, off the bat. *Come on,* I silently addressed those nameless deities, renowned for their capriciousness, *it doesn't have to be right now, does it? Give him a little time to get used to playing in the major leagues. . . .*

Matsui entered the batter's box amid tremendous cheering from the stands. "Mat-su-i! Mat-su-i!" came the chant from thousands of throats.

Hiroko and I gripped hands tightly and watched without a word.

The first pitch from Mays was a strike.

Matsui let the next pitch go by. A ball.

Followed by another ball.

"Mat-su-i! Mat-su-i!" The chanting was constant now.

Mays reared back and pitched. Matsui liked this one. He swung hard.

A foul ball, strike two.

The next pitch was another ball, a potential wild pitch blocked by Pierzynski.

The count was full, three balls and two strikes. Another ball would walk in a run for the Yankees. One more strike and Hideki Matsui would have failed the test set for him by the baseball gods.

The noise level in the stadium was off the charts. "Mat-su-i! Mat-su-i!"

There was the wind-up. The pitch. Matsui swung. I heard a sharp crack, and my throat tightened.

My wife, who had seen him hit so many home runs in Japan, leapt to her feet and shouted, "He did it! He did it!"

How can you know that already? I thought to myself a bit resentfully. After all, I was the one who knew about baseball. I had even played in college, before an injury ended all my dreams of a professional career. Yet it was Hiroko, who didn't know the rules of the game, and barely understood the strategy, who reacted immediately to Matsui's hit.

The ball, meanwhile, was heading for the right of the center stands, curving like a parabola, and the people there leapt up with both hands in the air. Was she right? Had he really done it? There was a huge roar, a tsunami of sound. Everyone in Yankee Stadium was on their feet, yelling and shouting, the TV announcer was screaming, my wife was dancing around the living room, and, seeing her, even our hard-to-please dog, Ice the Philosopher, was wagging his tail and barking in a most unphilosophical way.

And what of Matsui?

In the middle of all the pandemonium, a tight-lipped Matsui was slowly making his way around the bases. He stepped on home plate without once cracking a smile, only showing his white teeth when he slapped the hands of his teammates as they poured out of the dugout to congratulate him. Watching Matsui surrounded by his fellow Yankees, the words came to me as if from outside myself, and I thought, *This young man is a child of baseball.* Hiroko, who had been dancing around the room like a girl half her age, burst into tears. Even I was on the verge of tears.

Urged on by Yankees Manager Joe Torre, Matsui climbed back

out of the dugout and faced the roaring crowd, lifting his helmet in a shy salute to acknowledge the continuing cheers.

"Mat-su-i! Mat-su-i!"

Drying her eyes, my wife turned to me. "Do you think that now everyone there in America understands how talented my boy really is?"

Whenever Hiroko was in a good mood, helped along by one of Matsui's home runs or some other laudable feat of his, whether on or off the field, she would invariably refer to him as "my boy."

I confess that I sometimes thought of him that way myself.

AFTER the game, Matsui was surrounded by New York journalists who all wanted to hear his impressions. They could be summed up in a single word: Unbelievable!

The next day, news of his grand slam was all over the Japanese media. Articles about politics and the economy were relegated to a corner of the newspapers. Even in the City That Never Sleeps, the city that had seen it all, Hideki Matsui had made a memorable splash. As the *New York Times* put it, "Matsui already felt enveloped in the mystique and aura of the legendary Stadium where so much baseball history has happened. Actually, Matsui added to those feelings of invincibility by becoming the first Yankee to stroke a grand slam in his first game in the Bronx. He is now ahead of everyone from Babe Ruth to Bernie Williams in that respect."[1]

2

THE STAR,
MODESTY INCLUDED

For the rest of that April, Matsui played solid ball. His coaches praised him, and his teammates accepted him as one of their own. Even the Yankees' famously irascible owner, George Steinbrenner, pronounced himself satisfied with his newest acquisition. But some fans and sportswriters couldn't get that grand slam out of their heads. It was as if they expected Hideki to repeat it every time he stepped up to the plate.

There were no more grand slams, and only two home runs, the rest of that month and into May. Not that Matsui wasn't hitting the ball. No, he was getting plenty of hits. Only, they were all ground balls. From the season opener to May 20, he hit ninety-seven ground balls, the most in the American League. It was hard to believe that this was the same batter who had hit fifty home runs the previous year in Japan, the man whose sizzling drives had led to his being christened with the nickname Godzilla, after the fireballs that mythical movie monster shot from its mouth. Eventually, as the weeks went by, the harsh New York press attacked. The *New York Times* gave Matsui a new nickname: the Ground Ball King. *Newsday* was even more scathing, describing his swing as "a rusty gate." Then, as if he had only been waiting for the media to open fire, Steinbrenner trained his sights on Matsui and unleashed a verbal barrage. "All I know is, that is not the guy we signed in terms of power,"[1] said the man known as the Boss. Apparently, vice president of baseball operations Gordon Blakeley, the driving force behind Matsui's signing, had told Steinbrenner that, in his opinion, the Japanese slugger had inexplicably backed off the plate.[2] The New York press, smelling blood in the water, splashed Steinbrenner's remarks across their pages.

But even after the sharks started attacking Matsui, there was one man in the Yankees organization who recognized his talent and continued to have faith in him. That man was Manager Joe Torre.

On the first day of spring training in Tampa, Florida, Torre had been surprised by the size of the Japanese media contingent that was following Matsui around. The manager had realized that the burden of fame shouldered by Matsui was of a quite different order of magnitude from that of any rookie he had seen thus far. He worried at first that Matsui might rub his new teammates the wrong way by acting like a superstar before he had played his first game as a Yankee. But Torre soon saw what kind of young man this new player was. That first day, Matsui spoke to his fellow Yankees. "I want to apologize if any of the members of the Japanese press cause problems for you," he said. "If anything happens,

I would like you to tell me." Torre was surprised and impressed. Normally, players didn't express concern for their teammates with regard to the media. It was a welcome demonstration of character.

Even more welcome to Torre was Matsui's demonstration of his playing skills. He knew that Matsui was a power hitter and had been a home run champion in Japan. In Torre's experience, such hitters could be ego-machines who took swings at anything and everything, chalking up strikes galore in their pursuit of a crushing home run. It was almost an occupational hazard for players of that type. But Matsui's extremely compact swing allowed him to make quick adjustments to the ball, holding back when necessary and connecting for the kind of solid hits that a manager values far more than flashy home runs. With relief, Torre realized that Matsui didn't just hit with power; he hit with intelligence and judgment. As for speed, despite the nickname Godzilla, he was far from being a lumbering behemoth. Yet neither was he the fastest player on the team. Instead, Matsui ran hard and with the same intelligence that Torre had seen on display in the batter's box. Torre understood very well that base-running is not all about speed, and Matsui clearly understood that as well. His defensive play was similarly reassuring. He had a well-developed instinct for where the ball would be, and his agile glove and strong throwing arm made him a dependable fielder. Throughout spring training, as he studied Matsui with a manager's critical eye, Torre saw a fine all-around athlete, a man who understood the essence of baseball.

"He is very polite, and a wonderful man who gives his all in practice," Torre said. "He'll probably have a great season and become a leader of this team."[3]

From his extensive experience as a player and a manager, Torre knew that many players, blessed with an abundance of talent, played the game on talent alone, without really understanding the essence of baseball. It was rare to find a young man who combined talent with understanding. Derek Jeter was a young man like that. Now it must have seemed to Torre that he had found another.

What is the meaning of baseball?

That is a question I have spent a lot of time thinking about over the years. *Merriam-Webster's Collegiate Dictionary* provides a simple answer: "A game played with a bat and ball between two teams of nine players each on a large field having four bases that mark the course a runner must take to score."

Earl Wilson, a starting pitcher for the Boston Red Sox (among other teams) in the 1960s and 70s, called it "a nervous breakdown divided into nine innings."

Those are both good answers. Let me give you mine.

More than the most impressive personal record, more than a spectacular, awe-inspiring play, the genius of baseball lies in the fact that winning requires every player to do his best, not for himself and his place in the record books, but for the optimal efficiency of the machine of which he is a part. Not that baseball should be played coldly and without emotion, as if each player should strive to make himself into a robot. On the contrary! But it is a delightful paradox of the game, one of many, that a team with no superstars, just professionals playing at the peak of their abilities, can somehow become a better team than one composed of superstars out for their own glory. In baseball, at least ideally, the whole is greater than the sum of its parts, and the wise player will understand that and seek to find his place in the whole.

That's the difference between individual and team sports. How interesting would it be to watch the world's fastest man run a 100-meter race every day? Barring an accident, injury, or foul play, he would win every single time. The only suspense would be whether or not he would break his own record. True, that can be exciting, but the excitement of baseball is of a different order. Out of a million games, no two will ever be the same. The heroes change every day, and every day there's a new winner and a new loser.

It's a cliché to say that baseball is like life, but it's also easy to forget that clichés become clichés in the first place because they incorporate an element of truth. And the truth to this cliché is that in baseball, as in life, sometimes you win and sometimes you lose. Winning is great. It makes you forget the bad times and fills you with confidence and hope for the future. But the times when you lose are the most essential. Why? Because losing forces you to examine yourself and ask difficult questions. What did I do wrong? How can I do better next time? And most important of all, what can I do to help my teammates succeed? It takes a strong person to ask such questions and to answer them honestly, and then to implement the tough changes those answers require.

Honesty, strength of character, and perseverance in the face of challenging times: Those are the qualities I wish that every young boy or girl who sets foot on a baseball diamond could learn. A lot of them do. But there is no guarantee of it. Most boys and girls, regardless of their love for baseball and their understanding of the game, go on to do other things with their lives. Some young players continue in the sport and become professionals, blessed with talent and dedication yet lacking a deeper appreciation of the game. But the rarest of all are those who, at a young age, learn the true essence of baseball and try to shape their lives according to its demanding philosophy. That is the path of inner growth, of personal maturity. To such men—and women, for surely there are women who, if given a chance, would prove themselves capable of succeeding in the major leagues—to such people, baseball is more than a game, more than a job. It is a calling.

But can baseball really have such a profound meaning?

Ladies and gentlemen, I direct your attention to the great Lou Gehrig, standing before the crowd at Yankee Stadium on that sad yet inspiring Fourth of July in 1939: "Today I consider myself the luckiest man on the face of this earth. . . ."

FACED with his batting slump, Matsui demonstrated his strong character. Most players Matsui's age would have been shaken by the slump and the nasty sniping coming his way from the media and within the Yankee organization. But Matsui was apparently serene, smiling back at his teammates and silently going about his game.

One day, in the midst of this challenging time, Torre called him over. Matsui remembers the moment well. He wondered at first if he was going to be benched. In all the fourteen years since Matsui had started playing professional baseball in Japan, he hadn't missed a single game. His streak was at 1,768 games and counting. Perhaps he was looking to break Cal Ripken Jr.'s record. Nevertheless, Matsui was prepared to do what was best for his new team. If that required him to sit out a game, so be it. But Torre had other ideas. "I thought about giving you the day off," the manager told him, "but right now the team needs you. Defensively, you're irreplaceable. I wanted you to know that." Then he gave him a bit of advice on his batting.

Such is the managerial style of Joe Torre, a low-key, supportive approach that has led the Yankees to eleven consecutive playoff appearances, including four World Series championships.

In June, Torre's faith was rewarded. All the patience and hard work paid off for Matsui as his superb athleticism awoke from its slumber. That month he hit .469 (thirty-eight hits in eighty-one at bats) and had five home runs and twenty-seven RBIs. The player who had had fans scratching their heads, who had drawn the criticism of the tough New York media, and who had provoked the ire of no less a figure than George Steinbrenner was now the team's leading hitter, with the most runs batted in, at sixty. During the thirteenth week of the season, Matsui was chosen the American League's MVP of the week.

At the end of the first half of the season, the fans voted Matsui a spot in the All-Star Game, making him the first Yankee rookie to appear since Joe DiMaggio.

Going into the second half of the season, Matsui's performance remained steady. Instead of snarky nicknames, the *New York Times* was giving him glowing headlines:

MATSUI IS ONLY RELIEF THE YANKEES NEED (July 18, 2003)

MATSUI'S BIG SPRINT LIGHTS UP THE DAY (August 16, 2003)

In the midst of those day-to-day games, Torre bestowed the ultimate accolade. "Young players coming up from the minors can learn a lot from Matsui because he knows the game so well," Torre said in an interview. "Teammates and myself included trust him. He's a pro."[4]

Around this time, another article appeared that made me think the New York media had finally caught on to what it was about Matsui that set him apart. Written by Tyler Kepner, it appeared in the *New York Times* on August 22, 2003, under the headline: A STAR, MODESTY INCLUDED. At that time, the Yankees held a seven-game lead over the Boston Red Sox in the American League Eastern Division.

"The ability to hit for power has been just one of Matsui's tools," Kepner wrote, "and not his most impressive. . . . Where Matsui stars is in all-around excellence: in the field, on the bases, with his approach at the plate." Kepner went on to quote Torre: "When he came over here, you didn't know what kind of player he was going to be. If he was anything less than what he is, we aren't near where we are. He's given us such a lift."

Observed Kepner, "Like Derek Jeter, Matsui has shown a mastery of the fundamentals and rarely makes a mental mistake. Matsui started playing organized baseball in fifth grade, absorbing the game's nuances and sharpening his instincts through repetition."

Reading this article, I realized that, by the middle of his debut season, Matsui had already become a true Yankee, bringing much-needed stability to his left-field position, which had been played by seven players in seven seasons. I was quite pleased, of course, but what really struck me about the article was Joe Torre's perceptive comments. The manager had already been quoted elsewhere as saying that Matsui took his stardom humbly. Now, in Kepner's article, Torre showed that he had picked up on all the qualities that had made Matsui such a standout player in Japan.

While of course Matsui has phenomenal talent, he doesn't put on flashy displays or show off in any way. When he's not playing well, he never broods; he just quietly goes out there and tries to do whatever it takes to help his team win. There aren't very many young rookies capable of playing that way. At some point they show their immaturity, or their inexperience peeks through. But not Matsui. He seems to be gifted with an almost serene confidence. In my opinion, the source of this remarkable confidence, not to be confused with arrogance, is his modesty.

I don't think I'm in danger of any libel suits for stating that modesty is a quality in short supply in many of today's major-league players. In fact, the majority of professional athletes in Japan seem to be lacking in modesty as well.

Many Westerners have an almost stereotypical view of the Japanese as an excessively modest and polite people. It's true that in Japan one is taught to be modest from a young age. We have a proverb that basically correlates to the English saying "The boughs that bear most hang lowest," though the Japanese proverb refers specifically to rice plants, that staple of the Japanese diet, whose shoots bend low as the seedlings ripen and grow heavier. It is thought that the bent shoots resemble the bowed head of a modest person, and the idea is that, just as the bent shoot of the rice plant indicates a rich harvest, so, too, does the bowed head of a modest person demonstrate rich inner wisdom and strength of character. People will often mutter this old saying under their breath when they see a rich or powerful person behaving in a boastful or immodest way. It is no coincidence that when Japanese people meet, they greet each other with a mutual bow.

Yet not all Japanese people are modest. The military who started the Pacific War certainly forgot their modesty! And in the years since the war, as Japan grew closer to the West and took its place on the world stage as an economic powerhouse, the traditional values of modesty, never universally expressed, became even less common. Perhaps some Japanese young people came to confuse modesty with weakness, as is often the case in the West. Thus it was that Matsui's modest nature stood out all the more as the spotlight of celebrity shined upon him.

Modesty is a trait that evidences deep empathy for other people, as well as kindness and inner strength. It was Matsui's modesty, more even than his athleticism, that inspired me to write this book. How, I asked myself, could a twenty-nine-year-old superstar become such a pillar of modesty?

3

A PROMISE TO
HIS FATHER

At the height of summer in 1998, I received a phone call from an editor at a publisher in Tokyo. I was in my hometown. I had returned there to visit the grave of my younger brother, who had died in an accident at sea thirty years earlier. In Japan, during the summer holiday of *Obon,* the Buddhist festival to honor the dead, it is customary to return home to visit relatives. Legend has it that in the summer, the spirits of one's dead ancestors come back home, and I had gone back to my parents' house to be with family to welcome my brother's spirit. I was surprised that the editor, whom I had worked with before, had tracked me down during the holiday.

"We've got a great interview lined up for the magazine," he told me. "It's with Hideki Matsui of the Yomiuri [Tokyo] Giants."

"Congratulations, but why are you telling me?"

"He'll only agree to the interview if you conduct it. Well, what do you say? Will you do it?"

I wasn't sure I had heard correctly. "Did you say Matsui? From the Tokyo Giants? Hideki Matsui?"

"Yes, Matsui, the Home Run King. I'm sure you know who I'm talking about."

"Yes, of course I know who he is. Is there anyone in Japan who doesn't? But I've never met him. Why in the world would he have requested me?"

"He's read your books," the editor said.

"You're putting me on."

"No, really. He says he's a fan."

"I'm surprised," I admitted, still not quite believing him. "My books aren't that easy to read, you know."

"He's quite intelligent. Look, are you interested or not?"

"Can you give me a little time? This is all very strange . . ."

"Think it over, but I need an answer soon," the editor said.

I hung up the phone and went in search of my mother. I found her at the household shrine of my brother, where she was busy arranging flowers. "Ma, do you know the Tokyo Giants' player Matsui?" I asked her.

"Of course I know him. He's the one who hits the home runs," she answered. "He has a nice face. I like him."

I was about to tell her that Matsui was a fan of mine, but I decided against it. There was no way she would have believed me anyway. I was sure she would have said, "There aren't actually professional baseball players who read novels, are there?" And the truth is, up until that very moment, I had believed the same thing.

The previous winter, for an interview on a local television station, I had appeared with Ichiro Suzuki, who now plays for the Seattle Mariners, and a young pitcher who all the baseball journalists agreed was the new star player. I don't much like appearing on television, but a younger colleague of mine was the show's producer, so I made an exception out of friendship. After being kept waiting forever in the cramped greenroom, I was finally led into the studio. As he saw me walk in, the rookie made a face as if he had just caught an unpleasant odor and said, "Ugh, is there still more to shoot?"

"Looks like it," I said with a smile, hoping he wouldn't notice the blood rushing to my head and my right fist. I had met Ichiro before, so he immediately stepped in, explaining to the rookie who I was. I had no interest in saying anything else to the pitcher, but, for the benefit of my colleague the producer, I tossed him what I thought of as a softball question.

"What kind of books do you read?"

He looked at me suspiciously, as if I had just asked him a trick question. "What do you mean, *books*?" he asked.

"Well, novels, for example," I said.

"Novels?" He seemed unfamiliar with the term. "The only things I read are *manga,*" he said, referring to a kind of Japanese comic book.

I laughed, nodding toward the camera with a look that said, *No surprise there.*

Ichiro chimed in. "Why aren't Japanese novels printed horizontally?" he asked me as though I were some kind of authority on the subject. "I'd probably read them if they weren't printed vertically." He laughed, and I laughed right back.

But underneath the laughter, I thought to myself, *Who cares if*

*the characters are written right to left or top to bottom or even diagonally,
for that matter? What difference does any of that make?* And the answer, of course, is absolutely none. The important thing is what
the characters spell out: the words that are the building blocks of
stories and poems. Don't get me wrong: *Manga* is fine. But there
is more to literature than *manga*! The roots of Japanese literature
go back more than five thousand years, to ancient China, and
Japan has produced more than its share of world-class writers,
from Murasaki Shikibu, one of the first female writers anywhere in
the world, to Yasunari Kawabata, the 1968 winner of the Nobel
Prize for Literature, to the contemporary bestselling novelist
Haruki Murakami.

Perhaps it's different in America, but the sad truth is that the
majority of professional baseball players in Japan don't read too
many novels. This is not to say anything bad about the players—
in Japan, becoming a professional baseball player means earning a
large salary and becoming a big star. Who wouldn't want that?
When coaches discover boys who have talent, they send them to
the junior highs and high schools that have strong baseball pro-
grams. Once there, the boys play baseball all day long. College
scholarships are awarded regardless of academic performance. The
only performance that matters is on the baseball field. It isn't public knowledge, but there is even a high school that pays contract
money under the table in order to sign the most talented students.
If all the boys are doing is playing baseball from morning to night,
when would they have time to read novels? For that matter, when
would they learn how to read? Believe me, these days there are
plenty of professional baseball players who can barely read Japanese
at all. Okay, perhaps I'm exaggerating. But only slightly . . .

Anyway, it seemed that Hideki Matsui was an exception. Now that I thought about it, I remembered hearing somewhere that when Matsui had joined the Giants as the number one draft pick, straight out of high school, his grades had been excellent, good enough to get him into a top university if that had been the route he'd chosen.

That evening, I called Hiroko, who had caught a summer cold and hadn't been able to come home with me.

"How are you feeling?" I asked her. "Has your temperature gone down? How's the philosopher?"

I didn't want to come right out and tell her about the interview offer. Both she and her father were huge Giants fans, so I wanted to spring it on her as a surprise.

"Oh, by the way, this afternoon someone made me an offer to do an interview. Guess who with."

"A young and beautiful actress?" she said, teasing me.

"Hideki Matsui," I told her.

"No way," she said. "This is another one of your jokes, isn't it."

"It's no joke. And that's not even the most unbelievable part."

"What do you mean?"

"He chose me," I said.

"Chose you? I don't understand."

"According to the editor, Matsui requested me to conduct the interview."

"Hmm. Maybe he wants to teach you how to hit home runs."

It seemed Hiroko was feeling better. "Ha-ha, very funny. The editor said Matsui is a fan of my novels and that he really wants to meet me. Don't you think that's kind of strange?"

"What's strange about it? You're a wonderful writer. In addition to being a great athlete, Matsui obviously has good literary taste. I can't wait to call my father and tell him! He'll be so excited. So, when will you meet him?"

"Well, I didn't exactly agree to do the interview yet," I admitted.

"What's the matter with you? Call him back right now and tell him you'll do it."

"I don't know. It still seems a bit odd. . . ."

"Hmm . . . I wonder if my parents and I can come along?"

Hiroko has a way of hearing only what she wants to hear. But she holds a tight rein over everything in our house, so I decided it was best to give in and do the interview for the sake of keeping the peace. Besides, after getting her hopes up so high, it would be cruel to disappoint her.

The next day, after visiting my brother's grave, I went out to see the baseball field where I had often played as a boy. I had been working for several years on a novel set in my hometown, and some important scenes in the book took place there. As I reacquainted myself with the field, remembering the triumphs and defeats of boyhood, I found myself wondering what Matsui had been like as a boy. I realized that I didn't know a single thing about him that didn't have to do with baseball. I began to think of the kinds of questions I would ask him in the interview.

BUT despite the editor's urgency over the phone, the interview didn't take place until more than a month later. Matsui's schedule was full, and Hiroko and I had planned a vacation in France and Spain. But at last the appointed day came around.

It will surprise no one who has read this far to learn that Hiroko accompanied me to the interview. Once my wife gets her mind fixed on something, it is very difficult to dissuade her. In fact, I have learned over the years to not even try. Her parents, however, hadn't been able to come, so it was just the two of us.

Hiroko was very excited. She had gotten her hair cut and bought a new dress for the occasion. She had even purchased a silk tie to give to Matsui. Her excitement affected me, and as we rode in a taxi to the hotel where we were to meet him, I found myself unusually nervous.

"What kind of young man will he be?" I wondered aloud.

"Oh, everyone says that he's very well-mannered," Hiroko said breezily.

As we were led into the room, Matsui was already there, sitting in a chair by the window. Also present were the editor of the magazine and a photographer. When Matsui caught sight of us, he stood up right away and bowed politely. It was very pleasant to meet a young Japanese person who was so courteous in his greeting.

"How do you do?" he said. "I am Hideki Matsui. Thank you for taking the time to meet with me today."

"How do you do?" I said with a bow. "I'm Shizuka Ijuin. This is my wife, Hiroko."

"How do you do?" she said, beaming. "Please forgive me for tagging along."

Having introduced ourselves, my wife and I were silent for a moment.

We were both thinking the exact same thing: *What a gigantic person he is!* At six feet two inches, Matsui may not be unusually tall for an American ballplayer, but in Japan he towers over just about everyone.

Almost as if to apologize for being so large, Matsui gently shook my wife's hand. I thought for a moment that she might faint. But she controlled herself, and the three of us took our seats by the window.

I began the interview by asking Matsui about his childhood.

"How old were you when you started playing baseball?"

"I don't remember exactly, but my father says that he and I used to play catch when I was two or three years old. Then, since my older brother was already playing baseball, they let me join his team. It was a local youth baseball league. But since I was still small, I only dragged them down. The coach said it wasn't working out and asked me to leave the team. I was so ashamed that even when I grew a bit bigger, I didn't want to go back. But when I was about ten years old, a friend of mine was on that team, and he told the coach that he wanted me to play for them. The coach asked me to come back, so I started over again."

"So, if that classmate hadn't intervened for you, you wouldn't have gone back to playing baseball?"

He shrugged. "Probably not."

Soon thereafter, Matsui went on to junior high school, where he joined the baseball team and became captivated by the game. At the same time, his skills continued to improve. But the incident that would have the greatest effect on the kind of baseball player Matsui would grow up to be didn't take place on the baseball field at all. It occurred at the dinner table in the Matsui household. I'd heard about this incident from a number of sources, but even so, I only half believed it, so I took the opportunity to ask about it now.

"There's a story that I've heard from those around you—is it true that you have never once said a bad word about another person?"

"Ever since I decided that I wanted to be a baseball player, not once," he confirmed.

Slightly openmouthed (or so Hiroko tells me, though I was probably just smiling), I repeated my question. "You have never said anything bad about anyone?"

"No, never," he repeated.

Matsui had an earnest look in his eyes. And there wasn't the slightest tremor in his voice. He made this incredible assertion in the most natural manner imaginable. I glanced at Hiroko, who was listening to our conversation from a slight distance away. She nodded at me, gently saying with her eyes, *This young man is telling the truth.* The magazine editor and the photographer who were observing our interview, meanwhile, both wore expressions of astonishment.

"Why is that?" I asked.

"Because I made a promise to my father. I was in my second year of junior high school, and we were eating dinner at home. I said something negative about one of my friends. My father stopped eating his meal and said to me, 'You will not do something as coarse as bad-mouth other people at this table. Right now, I want you to promise to never again say another bad word about anyone. . . .' And ever since then, I haven't."

I listened to him finish speaking, and then I looked at Matsui's face once again. Somewhat sheepishly, he added, "To tell you the truth, I have absolutely no recollection of what I said about my friend at that dinner table."

Such a sincere young man, I thought.

"In your books, you have also said that one mustn't write slanderous things about people," he said to me.

"Yes, but that's on the page. 'The pen is mightier than the sword.' But make no mistake, I often say bad things about people in front of my wife, who scolds me for it. How is it, then, Mr. Matsui, that you never want to say anything bad? For example, when fans or sportswriters criticize your batting form?"

"The times I have wanted to say something bad"—he paused for a moment, then went on—"are too many to mention."

Matsui grinned broadly. Everyone in the room burst into laughter. I was relieved to know that at least he sometimes wanted to say bad things, even if, unlike me, he had the self-control to refrain from doing so. The man was human after all.

There was something else I was curious to ask him.

"Five other rookies joined the Giants at the same time you did. When the team introduced all of you at a joint press conference, the other rookies spoke about the records they hoped to break, the marks they planned to leave on the sport. You answered quite differently. You said that you wanted to be the kind of player that kids would want to come out to the ballpark to see. What made you say that? Have your feelings changed now?"

"My feelings haven't changed a bit. As a kid, when I saw Masayuki Kakefu play for the Hanshin Tigers, I became fascinated by baseball, and I always tried to play the game like him. I thought it would be great if kids could watch me play and feel the same way."

"Well, you have certainly accomplished that."

Matsui beamed when I said that. *What a warm smile,* I remember thinking. I realized then that any record Matsui would break would not be a mark of ego, a way to get into the record books. No, it was about giving kids someone to look up to. He was instilling in a new generation the same love of the game of baseball that had inspired him as a boy.

Another question I asked at that interview, little dreaming of its future significance, was whether he had any interest in playing baseball in America, in the major leagues.

"Hmm," was Matsui's reply.

I pressed him. "Don't you think you'd like to try to hit those big-time pitchers?"

"As a player, sure. If I had the chance, honestly, sure, I'd like to try."

That was the first time that Matsui ever said anything in public about how he felt about playing in the major leagues.

"Do you have any favorite major-league batters?" I asked him.

"I liked Mickey Mantle of the Yankees."

In retrospect, this answer, too, would seem prescient.

After the session was over, my wife took a photograph with Matsui for posterity, and he even autographed it for our hard-to-please dog. That photo, signed "For Ice, by Hideki Matsui of the Tokyo Giants," has become a treasured item in our home.

That evening, Hiroko and I went to our favorite sushi bar.

"I'm impressed," she told me. "Seeing that there is still such a wonderful young man here in Japan, it makes me think this country is going to be fine."

Hearing my wife speak with such emotion, the proprietor of the sushi bar said teasingly, "What's the matter, madame? You're speaking as if you've fallen in love. Have you met someone who has stolen your heart?"

"Yes. Today I met Hideki Matsui of the Tokyo Giants," she told him.

The normally reserved proprietor leaned forward with excitement, his dark eyes flashing. "Matsui? Really? Oh, I envy you! That guy is something special. He's different from all the other players, isn't he?"

"He certainly is," Hiroko agreed.

We left the sushi bar and walked out into the narrow alley. The summer moon was in the sky. Looking up at that moon, my wife said simply, "I learned a great deal from Matsui today. And it makes me feel wonderful."

As she looked up at the moon and waved both her hands, I knew just how she felt.

JAPAN'S NUMBER
ONE SLUGGER

In Japan there are currently twelve baseball franchises in ten different cities. There are six teams in the Central League and six in the Pacific League. Out of a total population of about 120 million people, there are an estimated thirty million baseball fans. That's a quarter of the population. So the ups and downs of the various teams have a kind of ripple effect that's felt all the way through Japanese society. Think of how New York feels about the Yankees or the Mets, or the way that Boston follows the Red Sox, and imagine an entire country like that. That's baseball in Japan.

Yet despite this, the loyalty of fans toward their home teams is not as deep-rooted as in the United States. This has been an ongoing problem ever since the establishment of Japanese baseball. And what is its cause? It's all because of the Yomiuri Giants.

It may be hard to believe, but out of thirty million baseball fans, more than twenty million of them are Giants fans. Perhaps this seems like an exaggeration, but I assure you it is not. Because the Giants were the first professional baseball team in Japan, they have won the most championships, and they are usually expected to be the best in Japan. You could say that they are seen very much the same way as the New York Yankees. When I was a boy, almost all of the young baseball players wore Giants caps, and almost all of the adults sat in the bars talking about the Giants' games and their star players. It may be that now the Giants' popularity has declined somewhat, but they still have the most fans by far.

At the time I first interviewed Matsui, the summer when I was so surprised and impressed by his poise and maturity, the Giants' legend had not yet begun to fade. For more than twenty million enthusiastic Giants fans, their top star was Hideki Matsui, the big hitter who had been attentively trained by "Mr. Giant" himself, manager Shigeo Nagashima. That is to say, there were twenty million fans who took such personal pride in each of Matsui's plays and home runs that it was almost as if a part of themselves had been responsible for these achievements.

When the magazine with my interview went on sale, I would see people in my neighborhood bar, and they would say to me something along the lines of, "So, you met Matsui, huh? You lucky dog! Hey, do you think you could get me his autograph?"

Every single person I met asked me about Matsui. Not one of them said anything about my novel that had been published that month. A novel that had taken me five years to write.

Nevertheless, I was in high spirits. I had a secret project that gave me great pleasure and satisfaction.

After the interview was over that day, Matsui and I had chatted about books.

"I understand that you like to read."

"Yes, I enjoyed it when I was a kid. But ever since I started playing baseball, I haven't had much time to read books. . . ." Matsui looked at me somewhat sheepishly. "Uh, may I ask you a question?"

"After all the questions I've just asked you, you can ask me anything you like," I told him with a smile.

"Mr. Ijuin, you played baseball until you were in college. How did you get to be a novelist? Did you read books even while you were playing baseball?"

"I didn't read that much, but I liked books a lot. It made my mother happy to see me read. Why do you ask?"

"I always get something out of reading, but I never seem to have the time. I think someday it would be great to have the time to read at my leisure."

"Hmm. But when your playing career is over, won't you want to be a coach or a manager?"

"I don't think I would. Right now I'm not thinking about when I stop playing. But it would be great to do some kind of work that involved books."

"I can see the headline now," I joked. "Former baseball superstar becomes librarian."

Matsui laughed. "The problem for me is knowing what books to read, especially with only a limited amount of time."

"Here's an idea," I said. "What would you think if I sent you a few books to read during the off-season? Not my own books, of course. These would be books for you to read for your future. . . ."

"I wouldn't want to inconvenience you," he said.

"It would be a pleasure. But if I'm going to send them to you, you have to promise to read them."

"I'll promise to try," he said.

"Fair enough."

So as that year's season drew to a close, I started to make a list of the books I would send to Matsui. It turned out to be much more difficult than I had thought it would be. *What kind of books should I choose?* I wondered. That day he had told me that he was reading an autobiography of Fujiko Heming, a deaf pianist who performed all over the world, so I chose several memoirs and critical biographies. Among them were a biography of Koki Hirota, the Minister of Foreign Affairs who had been strongly antiwar during World War II; a biography of Yoshio Ishida, president of Japanese National Railways (who had been deeply modest during his career); and a biography of the British Prime Minister Winston Churchill. For fiction, I chose Masuji Ibuse's novel about the atomic bomb tragedy in Hiroshima, *Black Rain.* A short-story collection by Guy de Maupassant. Historical fiction from Shuhei Fujisawa. And I included one collection of poetry. *Would he be able to read that?* I wondered. But then I thought of one of my old teachers who used to say that there's no point to reading unless it challenges you somehow, so I decided to include it.

Matsui called to thank me for the books.

"You can take your time reading them during the year," I told him. "Next year during the off-season, we can get together to discuss the ones you've read."

"Well then, I'll have to be sure to read them carefully," he said.

"That's right. Think of it like a literature course."

That year, the Giants didn't make it to the championships, and while Matsui didn't win any titles, he was one of the top three in almost every batting category.

The following season turned out to be fantastic for the Giants. Matsui sailed right along after the opening game, the Giants swept the pennant race, and they went on to become number one in Japan. Matsui wore two crowns as the Home Run King (forty-two home runs) and the RBI King (with 108), he was named MVP for the second time, and he won Best Nine and Golden Glove awards. That year, Matsui became Japan's number one slugger, both in name and in reality. And in our house, for the whole season, my wife was thrilled every time Matsui hit a home run.

5

A SIGH OF RELIEF

For Hiroko and me, middle-aged and childless, the appearance of
Matsui in our lives was magical. It was as though a sprite (okay, a
rather large sprite!) had breathed a kind of radiance into us. During the 2000 season, whenever Matsui would hit a home run, we
would jump and shout, and at dinner we would drink a celebra-
tory bottle of wine.

In that season alone, we opened forty-two bottles of wine. When
the Giants won the championship series, the television cameras
showed a close-up of Matsui's crinkled face as he and his teammates
hoisted their beloved manager, Shigeo Nagashima, onto their
shoulders in triumph. Matsui was named the series MVP.

Three hundred and sixty thousand people thronged the victory
parade in Tokyo's Ginza district. But later that year, the talk of the
off-season wasn't Matsui or even the Giants. It was the decision of

the Pacific League's top player, Ichiro Suzuki, to move to the major leagues. Ichiro was a sensation in Japanese professional baseball. Two years after he joined the Japanese minor league, despite leading the league in hitting, he still hadn't been moved up to the majors. Everyone agreed that his unorthodox "pendulum" batting style was to blame. But in 1994, his third year, a change in management brought Ichiro to the majors at last. Thus began his miraculous career. During that season, his batting average rose well above .400, and everyone went wild with the emergence of the first Japanese player to hit that high. What was more, Ichiro easily reached what had until then been the unattainable goal of two hundred base hits in one season. He was the leading hitter and was named MVP. For seven years running, he never surrendered the batting title. He was a three-time MVP, and he won the Best Nine and Golden Glove awards seven times each. There was talk that the only place for Ichiro to go was the American major leagues. He felt the same way, and he began to seek a foothold in America.

The first Japanese player to appear on a major-league team had been Masanori Murakami, who joined the San Francisco Giants in 1964, but it was not until thirty years later that the next Japanese player, the star pitcher Hideo Nomo, reached the major leagues. After that, as if a dam had been broken, Japanese players appeared one after another; all of them, however, were pitchers. The popular wisdom was that position players would have much higher barriers to overcome.

But a major-league scout decided that if anyone could overcome those hurdles, it would be Ichiro. Utilizing the posting system that allowed Japanese players to transfer to the major leagues, he was acquired by the Seattle Mariners, who had signed the pitcher Kazuhiro Sasaki the previous year. At the same time, the New York Mets signed Tsuyoshi Shinjo. With Ichiro's signing, the Japanese media amped up all their news about the major leagues, and NHK, the Japanese Public Television broadcaster, announced that they would be doubling the number of major-league games from what they had broadcast the year before.

The day after the announcement of Ichiro's major-league signing was splashed across the news, the evening tabloids began speculating about Matsui being the next contender for the major leagues. Of course, they didn't have a comment from Matsui himself. They based their speculation on the fact that in 2002, Matsui would complete his tenth year in the Japanese majors and would then be able to capitalize on his rights as a free agent. Faced with the fact that this speculation could allow things to get carried away, Matsui was forced to make a comment to the press.

"Do I want to try for the major leagues? I haven't given it any thought. What Ichiro does is his own business. I hope he does well in America. I have a tremendous amount of faith in him."

From that day forward, both the press and the Giants' parent organization, the Yomiuri Group, which was based around the Yomiuri newspaper, grew nervous about Matsui's attitude toward playing in the major leagues. Likewise, other corporations that owned professional baseball teams began to think about countermeasures to prevent their players from jumping to the major leagues. One result was the extension of players' contracts to multiyear deals. Before then, almost all Japanese baseball contracts were for one year only. But now the corporations no longer wanted to take the risk of signing single-year contracts.

During the off-season, the Giants offered to negotiate with

Matsui for a multiyear deal. But he politely declined, taking another single-year contract. Once again, there was much speculation in the media that Matsui had taken this contract because he had set his sights on the majors.

But at the press conference for his contract renewal, Matsui said, "The only thing I want to concentrate on is our team winning another championship next year."

Giants fans throughout Japan heaved a sigh of relief.

6

"MORE LIKE WHAT
A PERSON OUGHT TO BE"

On Christmas Eve of that year, Hiroko and I had dinner with Matsui at a sushi bar in Tokyo's Kagurazaka. The meal was my Christmas present to my wife. During the previous season, whenever Matsui had hit a home run, my wife had sent a congratulatory letter to Matsui's fax machine. From time to time, she would get a phone call from him thanking her for the messages. The two of them seemed to get along quite well.

This was a difficult period for Hiroko. Every week she paid a visit to the hospital where her father was fighting cancer, and as far as she was concerned, nothing gave him more strength than Matsui's performance. Father and daughter would watch the Giants games on TV together, and they were thrilled whenever Matsui had a hit. All kinds of people gathered courage and strength from Matsui. And of course, I was one of them.

That evening, Hiroko sat with Matsui at the sushi counter, the two of them drinking sake together in animated conversation. She seemed very much herself. And Matsui was laughing like a schoolboy.

"Right? Someday when we have the chance, we should all go together. You too," my wife said to me.

"Where are you talking about going? Hideki is very busy," I chided her.

"But I think we really ought to go," she said.

"Go where?" I asked.

"India," she replied.

"India?" I asked.

"Yes. We should all go to Mother Teresa's house and volunteer. Did you know, Hideki, that at Mother Teresa's house there are wards for the families of those who are 'on death watch' . . . ?" she trailed off.

My wife had a deep respect for Mother Teresa, and she often said that she wanted to travel to India to be of service there.

"You really shouldn't trouble Hideki talking about such things," I said.

But Matsui replied, "No, not at all. But I've never worked in a medical ward before. . . ."

"Don't worry. There are plenty of things you can do. For instance, I could make the beds or wash the linens and such. Hideki, since you're big and strong, you could chop firewood," she told him.

Matsui grinned broadly at what my wife said. "I could do that. That sounds wonderful. I hope we can go together. Mr. Ijuin, you should come, too."

Matsui's eyes were sparkling. My wife was nodding her head like a girl as she watched Matsui, who was going along with her plan. Frankly, I was taken aback by Matsui's generosity. Would I go to Mother Teresa's house? The thought had never crossed my mind.

I never would have imagined that this young man was Japan's number one slugger, who could bare his fangs and pounce, shattering Japan's pitchers with a single swing of his bat. By his mere presence, Matsui offered calm and solace to those who were around him. It was something I had seen and experienced many times.

What is his secret? I wondered that night as we sat sipping sake.

EVERYONE is fascinated by Matsui, but where does his charm come from? Was it because he was a star athlete? No, that wasn't it. I had met plenty of famous baseball players in my life. There were a number of guys from my high school baseball team who had gone on to become pro ballplayers, and my best friend from college had been the Giants' number one draft pick and had done well in the majors. Through my connections with these guys, I had met and talked with numerous star athletes over the years. And Matsui was not at all like any professional baseball player I had ever met.

For one thing, the majority of the professional athletes I knew were arrogant in one way or another. Pampered and fawned over from a young age, they had grown up knowing little of the real world. Matsui was nothing like that. He was not at all arrogant. On the contrary, he was quiet and well-mannered.

But that wasn't his secret either. I knew quite a few composed, well-mannered young men Matsui's age or even younger, and he stood apart from these men as much as he did from his fellow ballplayers. Curious to solve the mystery, I spent a long time quizzing the reporters who covered Matsui day-to-day.

Here is what one veteran journalist told me. "I've seen thousands of professional baseball players, but Matsui is different from all the others. When he made his debut, he didn't seem like all the other rookies. And every year, along with the progress in his game, I began to notice how this player was fundamentally different from all the other star athletes. Sometimes I would realize that this was what I was thinking even in the middle of a conversation with him."

"Yes, but what is it about him? Is it something to do with baseball?"

"No, it's more like what a person ought to be. It's odd. He's about the same age as my grandchild. I think he has a wonderful future ahead of him as an athlete. He's pretty amazing already. . . ." The veteran journalist smiled as he trailed off.

A younger reporter had a different impression. "Matsui? He shows up late. If you mention something about a pretty young girl, he's like, 'Where?' He wants to know the whole story. He's very affable, and there are times when he really seems like he's a friend of yours. But the main thing is that he treats us like equals. Athletes are people too, and so their likes and dislikes are going to come out when they deal with reporters, right? But he never gives an interview with that kind of personal emotion. That's why he's safe."

"Safe?"

"That's why none of the papers have ever run an exposé on him," he explained, winking suggestively. "There's nothing to expose."

But as it turned out, that wasn't quite true. After meeting with several young journalists, we all went out to a bar for a drink. I had written several novels whose subject was sports, specifically baseball, which fortunately for me were bestsellers, and some of these reporters had read my books and were as interested in talking with me as I was in talking with them. It got to be late, and as we were getting ready to leave the bar, one of the reporters muttered the words that had by this time become almost a kind of mantra with me: "Matsui really is different from all the other players."

He seemed a little drunk. But I was desperate. "What's different about him?"

"Do you promise not to tell this story to anyone else?" He looked me in the face.

"I promise."

"This was two years ago at the All-Star game. Matsui had played well in the game and was named MVP. You know what that means, right? Millions of yen in prize money. Big bucks. So right around that time, Matsui heard about this young girl who had been born with a heart malfunction, a condition that couldn't be fixed in Japan. There was nothing the doctors here could do, and she had been given six months to live. But it so happened that advanced surgical techniques available only in America might possibly save her. Of course, her parents wanted her to have this surgery, but when they added up the costs, well, there was no way they could afford it. Yet they couldn't just give up. Not when their daughter's life was at stake. So they started appealing for contributions on the street. Matsui heard about this and donated his prize money to the girl's parents. All without ever giving his name . . . A few of us reporters found out about it and wanted to do an article, so we approached Matsui."

"Wait. Why didn't you just go ahead and write the story?"

"Because Matsui had never given his name. We knew it was him, but we didn't have any direct proof. Besides, it's like I was telling you before, Matsui had always made a point of treating the press as equals, so it was just common courtesy for us to come to him first."

"So what happened?"

"He asked us not to write the article. He knew that if we really wanted to run it we would, and there was nothing he could do about it, but it was important to him that the article not appear. We didn't understand it. I mean, it wasn't like he had done anything wrong. In fact, he had done something very laudable. So we refused to back down. Finally, to make us understand, Matsui said something that I've never forgotten. He said, 'When you're a baseball player, people come to you with their problems, and especially when it involves children, I think anyone would want to help them. But I cannot give away money for just any circumstances. It so happens that I'm a bachelor, and I don't have to worry about money right now, so when I unexpectedly received the prize money, I was glad to be able to help. But if you publicize what I did, it will only make it more difficult for me to help others. I hope you can understand that.' " The young journalist shook his head admiringly. "Well, after that, as you can imagine, Mr. Ijuin, we decided not to write the story."

(By the way, I'm not breaking my promise by writing about this conversation now. When Matsui left for the major leagues, the young girl went on television and revealed how he had helped her. All of Japan knows the story now, but I think there are probably a lot of Americans who haven't heard it before.)

Just as I was shaking hands with this reporter and saying goodbye, he looked at me seriously and asked, "Mr. Ijuin, do you think Matsui will go to the major leagues?"

At that time, Ichiro had done nothing but dazzle since his debut with the Mariners. The Japanese media were starting to do stories about whether or not Matsui would follow in his footsteps once he became a free agent later that year.

"What do you think?" the reporter pressed me. "Should he go, or would it be better for him to stay?"

"Personally, I think that if Ichiro can do as well as he is doing over there, then Matsui would perform even better. I would definitely like to see whether or not Matsui's play would measure up in the major leagues. But I wonder what would happen to pro baseball in Japan if Matsui left for America. The number of people who follow the Giants would decrease by half. What does Matsui say?"

The reporter frowned. "Right now, we are banned from asking questions about the major leagues during interviews with Matsui. Honestly, we really don't know what to think."

"Hmm. Perhaps that means he still hasn't figured it out himself."

After leaving the reporters, I stopped in at another bar. The bartender there was a big Giants fan. Their record that year was not good.

"What are we gonna do about the Giants this year?" he grumbled when he saw me. "I get so depressed when they lose that now my wife is depressed too."

As I listened to the bartender's grousing, I thought about the story the reporter had just told me, and how Matsui hadn't wanted to publicize that he had given the prize money to the girl for her medical treatment. I certainly wouldn't have known about it if the reporter hadn't told me.

I thought about what happened to the founder of the Honda Motor Company, Soichiro Honda, and his longtime business partner, Takeo Fujisawa. Honda grew his business from a local factory that manufactured motorcycles to a corporation that was known as Honda Worldwide. Soichiro's strength was in engineering. The fact that Honda was able to break into the market, competing with such established motor companies as Toyota and Nissan, showed that, as far as the buyer was concerned, Honda's solid motorcycle engineering would easily translate into terrific automobiles. The Japanese people knew Soichiro Honda to be a man of integrity. Even as the company grew in size, Honda Motors poured money into various charities. That had been Soichiro's idea: to use customers' profits for the customers' benefit. It was his oft-repeated refrain. Every Japanese knows this part of the story. But what I was reminded of now was how, in 1960, Honda had secretly set up a committee to issue scholarships to young research students who were involved in science and engineering at colleges and universities throughout Japan. These scholarships were established "to support, endow, encourage fellowship abroad, and subsidize research, with the goal of participating in the promotion of science and engineering education." It was aimed at students who were engaged in research in the fields of math and physics, mechanical and electrical engineering, and materials science. At the time, Japan was still very poor, and the country was not able to support its young scientists. In that era, a young researcher earned a monthly wage of ¥30,000, or about $834.00. The scholarship gave them a stipend of ¥15,000, or $412.00. What was more, the scholarship did not require them to report on their research, nor did they have to repay the money. For these young scientists, it was a "gift from the science gods."

For the next twenty-three years, until 1983, when Japan had become a wealthy country, the committee continued to provide financial assistance. In 1984, declaring, "The wealthy era has arrived, our work is done," the committee was dissolved, and the remaining funds were contributed in full to an academic hospital. There have been 1,735 young scientists who have benefited from this support. From those students emerged some of Japan's most famous scientists and much valuable research. This "gift of the science gods" had but one mystery. The name of the person who contributed the funds was kept a total secret. In 1984, the scholarship recipients began to compile a report on the history of the committee's twenty-three years for posterity. For the first time, it was confirmed that the gods of the young researchers were none other than the president of Honda Motor Company, Soichiro Honda, and his longtime business partner, Takeo Fujisawa. The two had distributed ¥600 million from their private assets. When the media broke this news to the public, everyone who heard it was duly impressed with Honda Motors. It may seem difficult to understand why they had hidden their names, but the Japanese people thought of this as a virtue.

You can't expect to receive something in return for doing a good deed. There is a kind of shame in making it public or telling people what you've done. Just recently, in Japan, an incident occurred that illustrated this perfectly. A child fell from a train platform onto the tracks. Without hesitation, a man jumped down onto the track and rescued the child. Then he just walked away, without saying a word. Although many people had witnessed this act of heroism, nobody could identify the man. The child's parents, wanting to thank him, appealed to the media to help locate him, but despite all their efforts, the man never revealed himself.

"That goes to show you that we human beings are good at heart," people said about the incident. "Any one of us would have done the same, if we'd been there. . . ."

But I didn't think that was true. I think it took a special kind of person to jump down onto those tracks and then to walk away without a word. And yet, that man hadn't just rescued the girl. He had also given the rest of us a gift, helping us to think better of ourselves. Maybe the next time someone fell onto the tracks, that man wouldn't be there, but someone else, someone who had heard the story of the first man and been inspired by it, would find the courage to be a hero. To be, as that veteran journalist had said to me earlier, "more like what a person ought to be."

It had been quite a night out drinking. But though my head was getting a bit cloudy, I felt like I was finally beginning to understand Hideki Matsui.

7

A WRENCHING DECISION

The Tokyo Giants lost the championship in 2001. Matsui didn't have quite as good a record as he had the previous season. But something very significant happened during the off-season. The Giants manager, Shigeo Nagashima, retired, and he was replaced by the next candidate for manager, Tatsunori Hara. During his tenure as manager, Nagashima had been the biggest, most popular celebrity in professional Japanese baseball.

Manager Nagashima was particularly special to Matsui. When Matsui had been drafted onto the team, Nagashima himself had personally selected him. Most young Japanese baseball fans rooted for the Giants, but as a kid, Matsui had been a fan of Masayuki Kakefu, the slugger who played for the Giants' longtime rival, the Hanshin Tigers. There is a photograph of Matsui as a boy, wearing a Hanshin Tigers cap (see page 3 of the photo insert).

It's not an exaggeration to say that the course of Matsui's life was forever changed as a result of joining the Giants, all thanks to Nagashima. The fact that Matsui was now known to so many fans as Japan's best hitter was a direct result of being on the Giants. At the same time, as his batting coach, Nagashima had insisted on Matsui's rigorous training as a rookie. All baseball teams have a batting coach, but only Matsui was coached by Nagashima himself. The basis of Nagashima's coaching method was to create sharpness in his swing, which was why he insisted on such intense practice for Matsui. He corrected him during spring training, and throughout the season, after games, he would give Matsui instructions to practice his swing, both in the training area of the ballpark and at home. There were times when Nagashima would call Matsui at his home, or on his mobile phone, late at night unexpectedly, with some piece of batting advice from that day's game that he had been thinking about. When I interviewed Nagashima, I asked him specifically about this.

He said, "During the nine years that I was managing, no other player practiced more than Matsui. You can tell whether someone is practicing or not. There are a lot of players who will practice as hard as they can for one or two months. Once their game improves, they stop practicing. But that's no good. You won't succeed as a player unless you practice without missing a day, always focusing on how you want to develop your batting skills three or five or ten years in the future. Matsui was the only player who could do that. If you ask me whether Matsui is an agile or an awkward player, I'd have to say he's awkward. But in nine years, he's the only one who never missed a day of practice."

I asked Nagashima, "How did you know that Matsui was practicing his swing at home at night?"

He grinned and replied in a low voice, "I called him on his mobile phone late at night. If he had been out partying in a bar, I would have known by the noise around him. Matsui was always out of breath when he answered the phone. . . ."

A-ha, I thought. It may be hard to imagine in America, but in Japan there were a number of coaches and players who practiced at all hours of the day.

I digress, but forty years ago, the Giants' parent organization, the Yomiuri Newspaper Company, invited the Los Angeles Dodgers on a goodwill tour to Japan. At that time, Nagashima was the Giants' leading hitter. The Dodgers' president, George O'Malley, was taken out to dinner by the Giants' boss, Matsutaro Shoriki, and at the table O'Malley made a serious proposition to Shoriki to let Nagashima play for the Dodgers for two or three years. Shoriki declined. "If I sent Nagashima away from Japan right now," he said, "the number of Japanese baseball fans would decrease by half." If that had happened, though, Nagashima would have beaten Ichiro to becoming the first Japanese fielder to play in the major leagues.

One way to look at Nagashima's batting theory is to notice its similarities to major-league batting theory. It's basically to wait on the ball as long as possible and then follow through with a burst of power. Nagashima learned this theory during his days playing college baseball. His coach back then, Kuninobu Sunaoshi, had studied major-league baseball's batting style and had shown Nagashima lots of photographs. Incidentally, I was a junior player on the baseball team of a university that was affiliated with

Nagashima's, and I had the chance to be coached personally by Sunaoshi. He was so strict that he was known as "the Demon," and I can remember practicing fiercely to be able to bat the way he wanted us to.

Nagashima had been considering passing the torch to someone younger for several years. It was the Giants' circumstances that had kept him from doing so. He had had his fill of wearing a Giants uniform and just standing on the field in the ballpark. In 1980, at the conclusion of the final game of the season, not having improved the Giants' track record as manager, Nagashima was abruptly fired. When the fans learned the news, they were furious. Sales of the parent company's Yomiuri newspaper fell, and even the number of spectators decreased. After a long banishment, the Giants persuaded Nagashima to return, and the same year (1993) he chose Matsui in the draft. He then groomed Matsui to be the number one hitter in Japan.

In 1994, when they had won the championship, Nagashima had wanted to stand aside for the younger Hara, but the Giants, worried that attendance figures would again drop, wouldn't allow it.

Even after Hara became manager, the Giants convinced Nagashima to stay on as general manager and to act as advisor to Hara. Some say that one of his roles was to prevent Matsui from going to the major leagues.

For Japanese fans, the other thing that held their attention that year was Ichiro. His first year in the major leagues had been unbelievable. Leading the league in batting (.350), with fifty-six stolen bases and 234 hits, he broke the record for the most base hits by a new player. He was the perfect rookie star, winning a Golden Glove and a Silver Slugger award. And he was honored as MVP of the American League that year. Audience ratings for the major-league games that were broadcast in Japan skyrocketed. With Ichiro's appearance, baseball fans in Japan came to know the power and speed of the major leagues.

More and more people were saying, "Major-league baseball is much more interesting than Japanese baseball." Naturally, everyone was speculating about who would be the next major-league contender after Ichiro.

That same year during the off-season, there was another major movement within the professional Japanese baseball world. The players' association rose up to protest the owners and the pro baseball establishment with regard to players' employment conditions, annual salaries, issues with transferring, and so on. The players' association hired a lawyer to make revisions to the baseball regulations and demanded reform. Prior to that, the players had often complained about the same issues, but they had never followed through with their demands. The players had no solidarity, and since the employment conditions were status quo within the majors, they were forced to back down by management's strong-arm tactics. However, this time negotiations had heated up to the point where the players were prepared to go on strike. Baseball in Japan had reached the stage where both the concept and the organization needed to change. And the result of having been prepared to strike was that the players' association managed to achieve several of its objectives.

At the start of the off-season, players had begun to come forward and state publicly that they wanted to go out for the major leagues in America. In the midst of all this, the media's greatest attention had focused on the movements of Matsui, who the following year would complete his tenth year on the team and would gain the right to free agency. His negotiations for a new contract with the Giants began at the same time. They offered Matsui an extraordinary amount of money if he would sign a multiyear contract. But Matsui opted to renew for a single year only. Naturally, this provided even more fodder for a media obsessed with the idea that Matsui was headed for the major leagues. At the press conference after the contract signing, Matsui responded to questions about his intentions.

"I have to play each season with my back to the wall," he said, explaining his preference for a single-year contract. If Matsui signed for multiple years, it would mean that the Giants would be forced to keep him on the team even if he had a terrible season. By signing for a single year, however, Matsui removed the safety net. If he wanted to play another year for the Giants, he would have to earn that right. Thus, it was out of determination and dedication to each season that Matsui preferred to sign a single-year contract. But even after this explanation, the Japanese press continued to regard his move as a signal that Matsui intended to play in the major leagues after the 2002 season.

THAT year, as most years since I had come to know him, I met with Matsui numerous times.

In the early spring, I had gone out to Tampa, Florida, for research during the Yankees' spring training. There I saw a very interesting scene. At the end of practice on the first day of spring training, the manager gathered all the players as if he were going to give them instruction. Then he suddenly called out the name of

Baby Hideki, born on June 12, 1974,
was a joyous and happy child.

As a mighty toddler, Matsui looks like he's
going to lift up the tires by the axle.

At home with his father, Masao, who first
introduced Matsui to baseball

Matsui started off batting right handed
in the first grade.

Young Hideki with his brother, Toshiki, on a
family trip. Hideki is wearing the hat of his favorite
baseball team, the Hanshin Tigers.

Matsui taking the lead as captain of his team
in the Neagari Little League

At Nagoya Stadium, August 16, 1988. Eighth-grader Matsui's team
was the runner-up in the Central Region Tournament.

Ninth-grader Matsui competing in a relay race at Neagari Junior
High School, determined to catch up with the front runner

When Matsui became the team captain in his senior year of
high school, he set out to abolish bullying and hazing.

Matsui with his high school coach, Tomoshige Yamashita

Scouts were watching "Godzilla" Matsui's every swing.

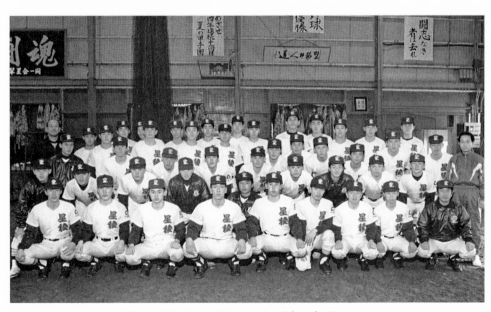

The 1992 Seiryo High School baseball team.
Matsui is in the front row, fourth from the left.

Matsui in the summer of 1991, wearing a
Los Angeles Dodgers cap

On deck in 1992, Matsui was a key player
on the All-Japan team.

Receiving the 2000 Mitsui Golden Glove Award, given to players with excellent defensive performance

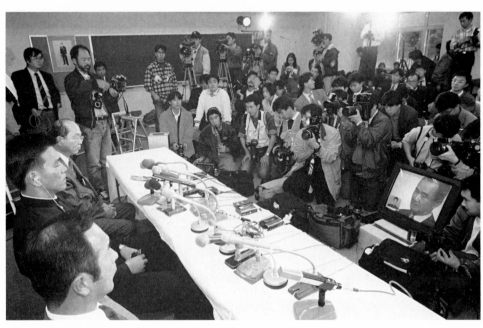

During a press conference at Seiryo High School after the draft, Matsui is staring at the televised image of his idol, Manager Nagashima, who helped bring him to the Yomiuri Giants.

While training in his hometown, Matsui is always
friendly with his neighbors.

Matsui with his father, Masao, at their favorite
restaurant in Japan

Delivering big for the Yomiuri Giants, Japan's most famous
and successful baseball franchise

Matsui had a cameo in a Japanese film that featured
the original Godzilla.

Celebrating the Giants championship win in 1996

Swinging away in his new New York Yankees uniform

Hideki Matsui—New York Yankee!

Matsui with teammate and friend Derek Jeter

Joe Torre gave Matsui great guidance on his
transition to the major leagues.

Matsui has great respect for the country of his team.

Matsui and Suzuki Ichiro having a laugh
at the 2003 All-Star Game

As a New York Yankee, with new members of his former team
and the future of Japanese baseball

one of the players. The other players shouted and clapped their hands. The manager said to the player whose name he had called, "You were late. Run around the bases once." Scratching his head, the player did as he was told and circled the bases. It seemed like a joke, but I had the feeling it was serious. I thought that this manager's leadership was fantastic. That manager, Joe Torre, was to become Matsui's biggest supporter in the major leagues.

"Matsui, I went to see the Yankees' spring training."

"How was it?"

"Wow, they are a wonderful team. They're extremely disciplined. Their manager, Torre, I think he's the best in the major leagues." I then told him in detail about what I had seen at spring training.

"Wow. The Yankees are different from the other teams, aren't they?"

Even while we were having this conversation, it really didn't occur to me that Matsui would go to the major leagues.

Most of the times that we got together, we didn't talk much about baseball. Maybe we would mention the Yankees, or he knew that I was working on the manuscript for this book. During the off-season, Matsui flew to New York, where he went to see a game at Yankee Stadium.

It was a game against the Red Sox. Matsui said, "I loved Yankee Stadium. It has a particular kind of atmosphere; the ballpark seems to have its own aura."

I don't know what it was that Matsui saw there at Yankee Stadium, but I thought maybe it was a good idea that he see some other ballparks as well.

I had noticed that Matsui seemed to be changing little by little. Perhaps it was that he was unsatisfied with the baseball he was playing—that is to say, with Japanese baseball. The change in Matsui had only become apparent to me since Nagashima had retired.

But still, Matsui wouldn't turn his back on almost twenty million fans, would he . . . ?

One night around this time, the two of us had dinner together. He wore an expression that I had rarely seen on him before. It seemed to be saying that his mind was somewhere else.

"Matsui, do you ever think about having a girlfriend?"

"Huh? Is that what you think is on my mind?"

"Well, at the very least, you weren't thinking about your batting, were you?"

"That's true, you're right. But I wasn't thinking about anything."

"Really . . . ?"

It wasn't like I didn't want to ask him when we saw each other, and even now I have no memory of what else we talked about. We must have made small talk. Unlike in the major leagues, during the off-season Japanese star players are incredibly busy. Autograph signings. Fan appreciation days. Various award ceremonies. Television appearances. All of this was at the bidding of the corporation that owned the team, in order to boost audience ratings on television. But whenever I would call him to ask if he had any time to spare, he would reply that he was available anytime. The reporters who regularly covered him, meanwhile, were receiving very different answers. They were told that Matsui didn't have any time available.

Even now, I still appreciate how Matsui found time for me.

Just before Christmas that year, Matsui also made time for my wife. In the car on our way to the same sushi bar where we always went, I reminded her, "Now remember, you mustn't ask him whether or not he's going to the major leagues."

"I know. But do you think my boy wants to go?"

Hearing what Hiroko said, I noticed the taxi driver surreptitiously watching us in the rearview mirror.

"That's why the subject of the major leagues is off-limits," I told her.

"Off-limits? But why?" she asked.

I didn't reply.

We had a light meal at the sushi bar, and after we parted from Matsui, my wife said, "My boy, something is bothering my boy. He's not the same as he usually is."

"What do you mean?" I asked her in response.

"It's like his attention is somewhere else. There were times when I caught him staring off as if he were by himself," she said.

I hadn't noticed, but Matsui probably did have something on his mind.

"It's just something that I know. We only see each other once a year, but haven't I always said what a wonderful young man my boy is? I just know something good is going to happen," she pronounced. Hiroko felt that she had a strong sense of intuition, and in fact I had learned not to discount her flashes of insight, even if she arrived at them by methods I couldn't fathom.

On the last day of that year, I visited Matsui, who was out in the country. There we talked a bit about what was on my mind. Matsui silently listened to what I had to say. I told him that just as there are four seasons in a year, there are ups and downs in one's life. I told him that there are times in a man's life that he has to make life-altering decisions, and only by considering all factors can he hope to make the best possible decision and move forward without regret. This may seem somewhat vague, especially to Americans, who are such plain-spoken people, but we both understood very well what I was referring to.

THE new year began, and Matsui's face appeared on the front page of the sports papers.

That year went by in the blink of an eye. I was busy with work and spent 150 days out of the year abroad on research trips. It had been a long time, but the novel I had been writing was finally published. It won a literary award, and now I was trying to write a different style of novel. Since I had been away from home so often, my wife had decided to get a dog. I don't know which one of us ended up loving that dog more. We named him "Ice," an English word which sounds the same as "to love" in Japanese. He was so small that my wife could carry him around in her arms. He was the kind of dog who trembled when he heard a noise, and it wasn't long before he was the master of the house. One afternoon my wife went out, and Ice and I were alone for the first time. I decided to read to him some lines from Socrates on virtue. As I was reading, the dog seemed to take on the moody attitude of a philosopher. Later that afternoon I showed him a photo of Matsui and then one of Derek Jeter. I wanted to acquaint him with baseball by introducing him to two of the greatest players; too bad I couldn't teach him how to play the game.

Matsui's performance was spectacular in 2002. He was unshakable as the Giants' cleanup hitter, and every game was a sellout. Matsui's playing was a sight to behold. As I watched him, I thought about how he exemplified what Nagashima had told me: that you won't succeed as a player unless you practice relentlessly, focusing on what kind of batter you want to become three or five or ten years in the future.

For the second year in a row, Matsui got the most All-Star votes from the fans. There were 1,298,046 people who thought Matsui was the best hitter in Japan. The Giants won the Central League pennant.

During the league's championship game, when it was almost certain they'd win, I told Matsui that I wanted to come see him play at the Tokyo Dome. He was surprised when I said that I had never been to the Tokyo Dome before, and he arranged tickets for me.

"Before the game, I'd really like to see batting practice," I told him.

"No problem. You should definitely come early," he replied.

Unfortunately, on the afternoon of the day of the game, there was a major typhoon in Tokyo, the likes of which we hadn't seen in decades, and the game was called off. The ballpark had a roof, so they would have been able to play; however, because of the huge storm, trains and commuter traffic were paralyzed. I arrived at the stadium just as the game was being called off. Ultimately when that game was rescheduled as the Giants' last game of the season, Matsui hit his fiftieth home run of the year.

But that night, instead of having the chance to watch Matsui's batting, I went out with him in Tokyo's busiest neighborhood. Because of the typhoon, the streets were empty. We went to a tiny restaurant that I knew well, and after dinner, I took him to a bar that was on the corner of an old building. I had spent many a drunken night at that bar when I was a struggling writer who couldn't sell his books.

"I didn't know there were still bars like this." He looked around, fascinated. The two of us had a drink together.

I felt like the person sitting next to me wasn't Hideki Matsui of the Tokyo Giants but one of the few people I consider a close friend. It was a very pleasant evening.

A LITTLE more than a year earlier, things had been much less pleasant. Even as Matsui and I chatted idly about the season, I remembered another quiet evening in September 2001. It was after ten o'clock at night, and I was writing in my office in our home in Sendai when Hiroko came running in. "I think something terrible has happened in New York City," she said.

"What do you mean, something terrible?" I asked.

"It's awful, a plane crashed into a building. I think there were two of them. . . ."

"Two planes crashed into a building in Manhattan?" I put down my pen and ran into the living room, where the television was on. Every channel was showing *CNN News.* Smoke was pouring out of the two main buildings of the World Trade Center, which were on fire. It wasn't clear whether it was an accident or terrorism. Soon we realized that another passenger plane had crashed into the Pentagon, and when the announcers said that they didn't know how many other planes were still in the air, it began to seem more likely that this had been a terrorist attack. Then one of the towers collapsed. Watching the people running all over the place on the television, my wife was moved to tears.

"This is so awful. Who would do such an awful thing?"

I could think of several terrorist groups who were hostile toward the United States. I did not know that the American president, George W. Bush, was in Florida at the time.

So this is how war begins. . . .

The thought vaguely passed through my mind as I watched the television. From that day on, people felt the strain all over the world. Thousands of people had been in the Twin Towers in New York at the start of their workday. Were there warlike groups out there who would commit such a merciless act upon civilians? I was glued to the TV all that night and into the next morning.

No country can allow the wanton slaughter of innocent people. Was there anyone this malicious in America? Where were the enemies responsible for this atrocity? The information was still unclear.

Twenty-seven days later, America launched an attack on Afghanistan after they had determined that the terrorist group Al Qaeda, led by Osama bin Laden, was to blame. It was the beginning of the "War on Terror."

"Another war has started? Many children are going to die," my wife said.

"You're right. And young soldiers will die, too. There has never been a time when there hasn't been war in this world. How is it that human beings can be so foolish?"

It seemed that mankind just couldn't stand it unless there was a war going on somewhere. No Japanese person can think of war without recalling the horrors our country visited on its neighbors and the United States in World War II, and the horrors visited on us in turn, culminating in the atomic explosions at Hiroshima and Nagasaki. Didn't people realize that war could only lead to the deaths of many thousands of innocent people?

BY that fall, Matsui had amassed a tremendous record. He had fifty home runs, 107 RBI, 112 runs scored, 114 walks, and his on-base percentage was .461. Matsui was riding high as the Giants roared into the championship series, which they won in four straight games.

ON October 31, 2002, the Giants' championship victory was the headline in all the morning papers. All morning the TV played scenes from the Giants' winning game and its aftermath, the raucous locker-room celebration as the players doused each other with beer. Twenty million Giants fans must have watched these scenes over and over with a sense of satisfaction. But Matsui had already begun to take action. Today was the day that he became a free agent. He was contacted directly by three people: the representative for the Yomiuri Group; the Giants' general manager, Nagashima; and Manager Hara. The corporation had already been involved in negotiations with Matsui during the regular season. They had told him, "If you leave the team, it will be a big hit to the Giants' power. But that's not all. It will have an effect on all of Japanese baseball. We ask you to please remain in Japan."

Matsui told me he listened without saying a word, and once

they were done he discussed his feelings with them. "I hope that you can understand how I feel," he said with bowed head.

Late that night, I got a call in my hotel room from a friend who was a news crew cameraman. Apparently one of the media outlets already had an inkling of Matsui's intentions.

"Sorry to call so late, but they say that tomorrow morning Hideki Matsui will hold a press conference at the Imperial Hotel," the cameraman told me.

"Really? I see, thanks," I said.

I hung up the phone and opened the window in my hotel room. An autumn rain was falling.

This is a very important day for Matsui. I'm sure that he made this decision all by himself. I hope he is able to sleep well tonight. . . . I said to myself.

The next morning, there were so many television cameras assembled at the hotel that it seemed like every station in Japan was there. They ran a special report on TV. Appearing onscreen, Matsui's eyes were red. He hadn't slept at all.

"I, Hideki Matsui, will now make use of my right acquired as a free agent, and I have decided that next year I would like to play in the major leagues in America." His voice may have wavered a bit at first, but the words that came out of Matsui's mouth were perfect. *Here was this young man, speaking flawless Japanese,* I thought to myself.

"This may be a betrayal for some Japanese fans. . . ."

You didn't have to say that, I thought at that point. But it was clear that Matsui was racked with guilt. And so he had to say it.

"Having reached my decision, I will stake my life on how hard I play." These words sent chills down my spine. *You're going to stake your life on this challenge?* In all the time I had spent with Matsui, I had never heard him say something that he didn't really mean, and I was astonished that he had thought it through to this point. It caused quite a fuss all over Japan. Everyone who had seen the press conference was impressed with every single word that this young man had uttered as he sincerely asked them to put their disappointment aside and try to understand his decision.

8

"POSTWAR JAPAN SENDS
ITS FINEST CITIZENS
TO AMERICA"

I got a call from Matsui in the evening after he made his announcement. "That was quite a press conference," I said. "You should go to bed soon, get as much rest as you can. You're going to need it."

The power of the Japanese media to shape public opinion is enormous. If somebody in the media states vehemently, "This is what is right," the Japanese people will believe that it *is* right, and it will tend to become a matter of public consensus regardless of whether it's true or not. I was very curious to see how the media would treat Matsui's announcement. Until now, the press had viewed him favorably. But would that attitude change following his press conference?

The first commentators responded sympathetically, impressed that a young man would be willing to stake his life on his career.

But I knew the media well, and I knew that it wouldn't be long before opposing viewpoints began to be heard. That's when I thought I would enter the fray. I figured it was the least I could do for Matsui as a friend.

The time came sooner than I had imagined. Two nights later, the phone rang in the hotel where I was staying, waking me from a sound sleep. It was an editor for whom I had worked many times over the years, who was now editor in chief of the bestselling weekly magazine in Japan.

He got right to the point. "Ijuin, why don't you write an article about Matsui for us?"

"But it's the middle of the night," I protested, only half awake.

"Yes, it's the middle of the night. So? Will you do it?"

"I'm sorry," I said, "but I'm turning down everything related to Matsui right now. If I were to make an exception for your magazine, what would the others think?"

"I understand what you are saying, but you're the only one who can accurately write about Matsui's emotions right now," he said.

"That's why, as I said before, I can't do it."

The editor's tone of voice changed. "Our magazine is the bestselling in Japan, Ijuin. Whatever we write about Matsui now will influence his reputation."

These words got my back up. "Are you threatening me? Because if you are, I can bare my fangs, too," I told him.

"N-No, that's not it at all," he replied hurriedly. "I'm a big fan of Matsui's. That's why I want what's best for him, and why I'm trying to commission you for this job. I have full confidence that you can do justice to Matsui. That's why I'm depending on you."

"Well, I'll have to get back to you."

I hung up the phone and lay there in bed thinking about it for a while. My perception that the editor had been threatening me had thrown me off somewhat, but there was a point to what he had said. Already in the media, little by little, people were starting to write things about Matsui being a traitor. I knew that it was going to get worse. With a sigh, I picked up the phone.

"When would you need me to write it by?" I asked.

"It's the middle of the night," the editor said.

"Yes, it's the middle of the night," I replied. "So?"

I got out of bed, took a shower, and went by taxi to the editorial offices. My article, which appeared the next day, was warmly received by those who didn't know what to think about Matsui moving to the major leagues. The owner of the neighborhood bar I frequented told me, "I've read everything you've written so far, but this piece was the best thing you've ever done. It brought tears to my eyes." Honestly, as a writer who labors for years over his novels, pouring heart and soul into every word, I didn't know if I should be pleased or angry at comments like these, about an article I had written in a single night. But that's how it is in the strange business of writing. You never know what is going to strike a chord with the public.

My article was titled, "Postwar Japan Sends Its Finest Citizens to America." Here's an excerpt:

It was impressive. And at the same time, it was sad. It was impressive that this young ballplayer had spoken for an hour and twenty minutes in such honest and eloquent Japanese, faithfully explaining the vagaries of his own heart. I had never experienced anything like it. It was sad that, thinking about all of his fans, taking his teammates into consideration, courteously thanking the Japanese baseball establishment, and following his own hopes, he was willing to stake his life on how he would play. This was not a laughing matter. Did he have to go that far? I had been watching Hideki Matsui for ten years. In those ten years, I had never seen him look the way that he did at his press conference. Perhaps it was that the young sapling was trying to grow into a big solid tree.

According to what he said, he had sorted through his thoughts on his own, coming to that day's decision by himself. In this day and age of weak-minded Japanese who cannot even stand up for themselves, is a twenty-eight-year-old a young man or a grown adult? Not that long ago, there is no question that he would have been considered a grown man. During the Meiji Era [1868–1912], the people in whom we took pride, whom we sent out into the world as representatives of the Japanese people, were all the same age as Matsui. I had thought about that as I listened to him at his press conference.

Several years earlier, I had been fortunate enough to have the chance to speak with Matsui.

"How important is it to you to appear in every game?"

"It's not that it's so important to me, myself, it's that tickets to Giants games can be very difficult to get. I think about the kids who are there and only get to see one game the whole year. Some of those kids sitting in the stands may be there to see me play. That's why I want to play in every game," Matsui said, his lips in a tight line.

I found Matsui utterly charming. I was not a Giants fan, but I was a big fan of baseball.

"Do you think there is a god of baseball?"

"That I don't know, but I do believe in God."

Matsui had said that he wanted to handle the negotiations in his move to the major leagues alone, without an agent. He must have been thinking about other young players who were likely to try to go over to the major leagues after he did and wanted to carve a new path for them. I have no idea if it will be easy to do, but wherever there are talented new players in Japanese pro baseball, a business is created out of the speculation of the people who swarm around them. There's no way to know how many new recruits have been consumed by the lure of money. Matsui didn't want that to happen to young players, and so he was trying to open the door to the major leagues all by himself.

Articles have already appeared in the Japanese media about Matsui's performance in the major leagues. They are sure that Matsui will succeed the way that Ichiro has. But there certainly isn't any guarantee. In professional sports, everything is based on results. Still, I want to see him play to his highest potential, and I hope he will have a fantastic career in the major leagues.

I thought about these things as I watched his press conference. Toyota, Sony, Honda . . . I realized that, of all the Japanese, it was always our finest citizens whom we had sent to America. Next spring, I look forward to seeing the boyish smile on the face of our affable Matsui, standing on the field of a major-league stadium.[1]

Not even Matsui could have imagined how busy he would become after making the announcement that he wanted to move to the major leagues. First of all, there was the question of which major-league teams he might be interested in playing for, and which teams had a reciprocal interest in him. He still didn't understand why it was so important to hire an agent as his representation. Next, the Giants' parent organization, the Yomiuri Group, was proving unusually persistent in their efforts to retain Matsui. They were attempting to negotiate what in Japan is known as a rental transfer, when a player is loaned to another team while fully maintaining his contract with the original team. American baseball fans may be unfamiliar with this system, but it is often employed by Japanese soccer teams. If Team A is having a bad season, for example, it might rent out its top player to the more successful Team B in order to let that player play more games in the playoffs. Baseball organizations had never used the rental-transfer system before, but Yomiuri was so determined to hold on to Matsui that they were willing to change the way baseball was played in Japan. On top of all this, each of the media companies besieged Matsui for interviews. It's no surprise that, until the day he left Japan, he wasn't able to do any sort of training. This could have caused quite a crisis for Matsui in his debut year.

9

WAR, PEACE, AND
GROUND ZERO

Hideki Matsui was born in Ishikawa prefecture on June 12, 1974, the second son of Masao and Satoko Matsui. At eight pounds, seven ounces, he was exceptionally large for a baby born in Japan. His father named him "Hideki"—the first character of his name, *hide,* means "to excel," and the second character, *ki,* means "joy"— because he wanted his son to attain great skill in life and to be happy.

In order to try to understand how Matsui's parents raised their son to be a superstar, we need to go back thirty-two years before he was born, to the birth of his father, Masao. On that day, Masao's father, Kanari, heard a voice from the Buddhist god of his religion. "That baby is not yours," the voice told him. "That child is a gift from God." When Masao was ten years old, Kanari told him about what he had heard. But of course, Masao could only have assumed that his father was speaking nonsense.

Masao graduated from college and went on to become a computer engineer. He was still a bachelor at twenty-eight, when seemingly out of nowhere an old local woman named Miyo Matsui, who was from the same Buddhist sect as Masao's father, came calling on him. From the first time Masao met the old woman, he felt a strange sense of familiarity with her and was drawn to her. The feeling was mutual. In fact, Miyo adopted Masao into her family, and he took the last name Matsui as his own. This is a traditional practice in Japan when a family without a son wishes to ensure the continuance of the family name.

Ever since she was a young girl, Miyo had possessed a strange power—she would pray for the sick, and they would heal—and for this reason she was revered by many people. Miyo's husband, Yosamatsu, had been hugely successful in the textile business as a young man and had amassed a vast fortune. At one time, the couple began talking about how they wanted to do something for the people of the world, and they decided to start using their personal assets for work that would spread the beliefs of their religion to others.

One day, when Masao was helping Miyo with various things, her beautiful young daughter, Satoko, appeared at her side. Masao and Satoko fell for each other right away, and they were soon married. As if she had been waiting to assure herself of their marriage, Miyo died shortly thereafter. But just before her death, Miyo said to Masao and Satoko, "You will be blessed with two sons. And someday, those two boys will work hard to spread the Matsui name, and many people will know it, and you will rejoice."

As I said, Masao's father, Kanari, and Miyo were of the same religion, the Jodo-Shinshu, or True Pure Land, sect of Buddhism, which descends from a form of Buddhism that has been practiced in Japan for more than a thousand years. This sect is based on the principle that everyone can achieve salvation by simple but absolute devotion to the Buddha. The sect had created its own concept of salvation, and it did not accept money from its practitioners.

When you consider the message that Kanari received about his child being a gift from God, and Miyo coming into Masao's life, adopting him, and introducing him to Satoko, this may seem like a made-up story. But the Japanese people have always been strongly religious, and such stories, while they may seem strange to Westerners, do not strike most Japanese people as at all unbelievable. Traveling throughout Japan, one sees countless shrines and temples dedicated to the gods. Every village has places that are considered sacred, where the people pray to the gods and are protected by them. If you look back on Japan's history, there are more than a few legends of so-called "children of the gods," emperors and leaders who saved the country from disasters and crises.

I am not trying to say that Matsui is really a child of God, at least not any more than we all are. He does not possess supernatural abilities—even though, watching him on the baseball field, I often felt that he did. But something about his upbringing allowed him to reach a potential that few children ever achieve.

Hideki and his older brother, Toshiki, were raised with great love and respect by their parents. The two brothers got along well, and Hideki, four years younger, always wanted to do everything that Toshiki did. In fact, the reason why Hideki started playing baseball is because his brother was already hooked on the sport. Toshiki was good at the game, and in order to try to match him, Hideki says that they would play catch until the sun went down.

The brothers lived in the same house and ate dinner every night with their beloved grandfather, whose own dignified attitude toward how to live one's life had a tremendous influence on them. One of the most important lessons that he imparted to them was never to tease or bully anyone else.

For the past twenty years or so in Japan, bullying in elementary and junior high schools has been a problem. There are probably the same issues in America. This became a problem for Matsui around the time when he was in junior high school. In the Japanese school system, students report to their homeroom teachers, and various troubles and issues are resolved within this classroom. When Matsui was in his last year of junior high, due to a change in the way the classes were organized, one of the teachers requested that Matsui be in her class. Apparently, Matsui's influence was such that, as long as he was in the classroom, incidents of bullying dropped to zero. Nor was his positive influence restricted to the school day. After classes, Matsui would tutor students who required special help. "I've never had a kinder student," his homeroom teacher said.

Characters of junior high school age have played important roles in some of my novels. Because of this, I have been asked many times by the media to give my opinion on the problem of bullying in schools, and I was once invited to speak on a panel at a symposium on the subject. In my research to prepare for this appearance, I discovered a passage that Hideki Matsui had written about bullying. Here it is:

To all those who have ever been bullied, God will never forsake you. You must try to be brave and confront this suffering with courage. I know it may be difficult to tell your parents or teachers or friends about being bullied, but if you gather your strength and talk to them, I believe things will only improve. The least courageous thing would be to leave your own life unfulfilled. The reason why you are alive is that God decided that you are meant to be here in this world. But if you still cannot find the courage, please let me know. You can write me a letter because I want to help you. If there is anything that I can do for you, we will work it out together. I hope you will have a wonderful life.

Hideki Matsui[1]

When I mentioned to Matsui that I had seen this message of his, he told me that he has received many letters in response. He said that he always makes sure to reply to them.

"Bullying someone else is the most dishonorable thing a person can do," he said.

"I agree with you," I said.

"Like when a group gangs up on one kid. When a group gets together, even a child understands the power they can have. When someone else has power over you, they can make you feel as if you are a bad person. This doesn't only apply to children. When it happens between adults, that's how wars start. That's why I think war is man's biggest folly, his most dishonorable act."

"Hmm. So you see war as a kind of bullying?"

"I hate war," he said. "In the countryside where I grew up, there are graves of people who died in the last war. War is foolish, indeed. I like to think that by playing baseball, I am sending the world a message of peace. Once the Americans and the Japanese were enemies, but now we are united by our love of this sport. It's too bad that all conflicts can't be solved on the baseball field," Matsui said with a serious expression.

AFTER Matsui signed with the New York Yankees, we had one last dinner together in Japan before his contract started.

"Congratulations," I told him. "You're joining the team of one of your heroes, Mickey Mantle."

"Thank you. I hope it goes well," he said.

"It's great that New York will be your new home. It's a fantastic city, with plenty of museums and concert halls that I'm sure you will enjoy."

He nodded. "I keep thinking about the terrorist attacks on 9-11. A lot of people were killed that day. Many children lost their parents."

"You'll have to hit a lot of home runs to give those kids courage," I told him.

"That would be great, wouldn't it?"

On January 9, 2003, when Matsui arrived in New York to begin his new career, there was a huge blizzard. As soon as he got to his hotel, the first thing he said to his interpreter, Isao Hirooka, was, "Let's go to Ground Zero."

It was an unscheduled activity, but Isao soon grasped what Matsui's intentions were. The two of them headed downtown to Ground Zero by car. For one hour, in the middle of the snowstorm, Matsui stood and stared at the remains of that tragic event. When I heard about this, once again I saw how much Matsui hated war and how he hoped that those who had perished would rest in peace.

10

THE MENTORS
BEHIND MATSUI

I don't think I'll ever forget the night of October 16, 2003.

The Yankees were playing the Boston Red Sox at Yankee Stadium in the seventh game of the American League Championship Series. At the start of the postseason, the Yankees had defeated the Minnesota Twins 3–1 to win the division series, and now they were competing against the Red Sox. The teams rivaled each other in strengths, and with three wins and three losses each, they were battling it out in the final game of the series. There had been a scuffle during Game 3 of this playoff series when the seventy-two-year-old Yankee bench coach, Don Zimmer, had made a dash for the Red Sox pitcher, Pedro Martinez, and Martinez had flung Zimmer away from him by the head, injuring Zimmer and starting a major ruckus.

Game 7 started with the ace pitchers from both teams. For the

Yankees, that was Roger Clemens, and for the Red Sox, it was Martinez. Martinez was in fine form through the seventh inning, allowing only two solo home runs, both by Jason Giambi. On the other hand, the Red Sox lineup got to Clemens, who gave up four runs before leaving the mound. At the top of the eighth inning, David Ortiz hit a home run for the Red Sox, bringing the score to 5–2 and seeming to assure a victory for Boston.

But then, with only one out in the bottom of the inning, the tried-and-true Yankee players launched a fierce comeback rally. Derek Jeter hit a double, followed by a timely hit single by Bernie Williams. As Jeter made it home safely, he appealed to the next batter, Matsui; they were counting on him. As if in response, Matsui sent a line drive straight to right field. Since a spectator touched the ball, it was called a ground rule double, and Williams advanced to third base.

Next up, Jorge Posada sent a hit out to center field. The second baseman, shortstop, and center fielder all went after the ball. At that moment, Matsui, the runner on second base, took off running, sensing it would be a hit. Running with all he had, Matsui struck an unusual victory pose as he reached home plate, waving his fist as he took his last step.

Watching these four hits in a row, once again I could appreciate the wonder of the game of baseball. When players do their best in the name of victory, they can turn around a game that seemed like it was already over. The game went into extra innings, and, in the bottom of the eleventh, Aaron Boone sent the Yankees to the World Series with what is known in Japan as a "sayonara home run"—that is, a home run that clinches the game in the bottom half of the last inning.

As I watched this game in Japan, I wondered how many people who had helped raise Matsui were rejoicing at that moment. I would have bet that the happiest of them all was his father, Masao. The relationship between Masao and Hideki was a bit different from the traditional father-son relationship. The long-established custom in Japan is that the child obeys whatever his father says, immediately and unconditionally. But ever since Toshiki and Hideki were children, Masao had treated them as though they were his equals. A good example of this is the way he never simply called them only by their first names; he always spoke to them respectfully, even formally, using the honorific, Hideki-san or Toshiki-san.

And when one of the two brothers did something wrong or got into trouble, their father wouldn't mindlessly punish them but instead always asked why they had done whatever it was. If the boys already understood their mistake, that would be the end of the discussion. But if they didn't, their father would say, "Here's what I think . . . ," and they would talk through the problem until they had resolved it together. Even when punishment was necessary, as it sometimes was, Masao never raised his hand to his children, something that was quite common in Japanese parenting at the time.

That's not to say that he had a laissez-faire attitude. His discipline took the form of sayings along the lines of "Always greet people properly," "You can do whatever you like as long as it doesn't interfere with or cause problems for others," and "You should resolve your problems on your own." It's easy to understand the nature of Masao's relationship with Hideki by reading the 216 letters he wrote to his son in the ten years from 1994 through 2004. Published in Japan, they have become a model of the ideal father-and-son relationship. The letters are filled with a father's love for his son, but at the same time there is a kindness in the words he has written that seems directed more to one of his close friends. The letters are characterized by Masao's expressions of love for his son during various times of adversity, when he has fallen into a slump, or when he is injured. But in dispensing his advice, Masao has never once disagreed with any of Matsui's beloved baseball mentors.

Matsui has told me that he feels like he has been blessed with his mentors. Even I have to admit that it seems like each of Matsui's mentors appeared at key moments throughout his life. Take his junior high school coach, Michihiro Takakuwa, for example. Takakuwa himself had gone from Seiryo High School, which in Ishikawa prefecture was locally renowned for baseball, to the prestigious Komasawa University in Tokyo, where he had been among the elite on a baseball team that won two league championships.

When Matsui joined the baseball team in junior high, some may have thought that he was a chubby kid. The first thing Takakuwa did was force Matsui to run in order to completely transform his physique and develop his agility so that he could play baseball. There were even times when he hit him in the face with his open hand. But despite such grueling training, Matsui never complained. Soon Matsui stood out from the rest, and the junior high school team manager, Hiroshi Miyata, made him a starting player while he was still a first-year student. The only time Takakuwa publicly scolded Matsui was when he threw his bat on the ground in anger and frustration after striking out.

"Anyone who doesn't show respect for equipment doesn't deserve to play baseball," Takakuwa admonished him.

When Matsui graduated to high school, he attended Takakuwa's alma mater, Seiryo High School. Hideki's mother, Satoko, worried that his days would be filled with only baseball and wanted him to go to the same school as his brother, Toshiki. But Matsui chose Seiryo, and there he met Tomoshige Yamashita, the high school team's manager. The three years he spent with Yamashita signified the beginning of Matsui's efforts to play baseball in earnest.

To thank Yamashita for taking Matsui onto the baseball team, Masao went to see him and, bowing his head, said to him, "I entrust Matsui to you for the next three years."

Every Japanese high school baseball player has the same grand objective: the national championship, which, ever since 1977, takes place twice a year, in the spring and the summer, at Koshien Stadium. The spring tournament is a national invitational, where teams are selected from among the 4,100 schools in the country, and the summer tournament consists of teams that have beat out other teams in their prefecture. All of the games are broadcast on national television, and baseball fans all over Japan watch the competition closely. Koshien Stadium is home to the professional baseball team the Hanshin Tigers, and during the summer tournament, they clear out on a two-week-long road trip. Many famous players have been produced from these tournaments. Japan's Home Run King, Sadaharu Oh, Hideki Irabu, Kazuhiro Sasaki, Ichiro Suzuki, Shigetoshi Hasegawa, and, of course, Hideki Matsui all played there. Led by Manager Yamashita, Seiryo High School made regular appearances at Koshien. One of the reasons why Matsui chose Seiryo for high school was because it had always been his dream to appear on the Koshien stage. The training in high school was so intense that there was no comparison with the regimen he had followed in junior high. From morning until night, whenever they weren't in class, the players' lives were all about baseball and only baseball. But the results of all his training were that Matsui was a starter from his first year, and he made four appearances at Koshien. He earned his nickname during his second year, when a journalist who saw him hit a home run dubbed him "Godzilla" in an article he wrote, comparing the awesome power of the young man's blast with the fireballs that Godzilla shot from his mouth.

The summer of Matsui's third year, something happened at Koshien Stadium that shocked people throughout Japan. When Matsui entered the batter's box for each of his five at bats, the opposing team, following its manager's orders, gave him an intentional walk. This was the first time that anything like this had ever taken place at Koshien. The ballpark was thrown into an uproar. In the end, Matsui's team lost by two runs. The media criticized the other team manager for his strategy. When young people are playing baseball, it was widely felt, there should be other priorities than just winning at all costs. But as a result of this incident, Matsui's name echoed throughout the country. Every professional baseball organization fought to choose him as their top draft pick.

Later, Manager Yamashita spoke of Matsui. "In my whole career, I have never seen a batter like Matsui," he said. "And I doubt that I ever will again. What was most amazing about Matsui wasn't just his strength as a hitter, it was that he worked so hard. His tenacity to improve his game with practice was most impressive. In three years, there wasn't a single day when he slacked off on his training. That's why his teammates thought so highly of him."[1]

It seems to me that Yamashita's moral education must have had a powerful effect on Matsui and the other young men on the Seiryo team. Here is some of the advice that Yamashita hung on the locker room walls for his players to ponder:

If you can change your mind, you can change your actions.

If you can change your actions, you can change your habits.

If you can change your habits, you can change your character.

If you can change your character, you can change your destiny.

I once asked Matsui about Manager Yamashita, and he rattled off these lines to me. Matsui felt that he was indebted to Yamashita for having opened up the path of his career from that of a student to that of a professional baseball player. He told me that Yamashita had been like a father figure on the field and had helped him to develop the razor-sharp mental capacity that he needed to succeed in the majors.

Matsui's entry into professional baseball was, as I've already written, all due to meeting Shigeo Nagashima. He had been the biggest superstar in Japanese baseball, and he was making his comeback as the Giants' manager after thirteen years away. I think it was both of their fates that he chose Matsui in the draft, bringing him onto the Giants team.

With the relentless training habits that he had learned from Yamashita, Matsui now moved on to the next level with an even stricter mentor. Even now, after all these years, if Matsui has a slump, Nagashima will call him up in New York to give him batting advice.

Matsui has often said, "I am who I am today because of the

amazing mentors and teammates I have had. If I had not met any single one of them, I wouldn't be the same person."

Finally, when he reached the major leagues and met the famous Joe Torre, Matsui found the mentor who understood him better than anyone. And what is more, he became teammates and friends with the fantastic Derek Jeter.

Some say that life is about the people you meet. When I trace the path that Matsui's life has taken, I am utterly convinced of this.

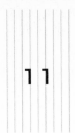

11

TO THE SPONSOR
THEY HAVE NEVER MET

Having defeated their longtime rivals, the Boston Red Sox, in a huge upset, the Yankees hoped to keep the momentum going as they faced the Florida Marlins in the 2003 World Series. Manager Torre entrusted Matsui with the cleanup position for the series. Before the playoffs began, the Yankee great Reggie Jackson, famed as "Mister October" due to his amazing performance in postseason games, had said that Matsui would probably be the "Mister October" for 2003.

Although Matsui played well in Game 1 of the World Series, with two hits in three at bats, the Yankees lost 3–2.

In Game 2, Matsui hit a three-run homer in the first inning, and the Yankees won 6–1.

Game 3 shifted to Miami, where the Yankees were again victorious by the score of 6–1. They now had just two games to win, and they would be world champions.

I was in Miami for Game 4. Roger Clemens was the starting pitcher that night. Since the media had been saying that it would probably be Clemens's last time pitching, the stands were filled with fans carrying their cameras, and every time Clemens threw a pitch, the stadium sparkled with flashes. After the first half of the seventh inning, when Clemens threw his last pitch and came off the mound, the crowd in the stands, Yankees and Marlins fans alike, stood and applauded. The applause continued, and when Clemens faced the standing ovation, took off his cap, and waved it at the crowd, the cheers grew even louder. The Yankees tied the game at 3–3 in the top of the ninth inning, but they lost in the bottom of the eleventh when Alex Gonzalez hit a home run. The series was now tied, two games apiece.

The Yankees lost again in Game 5. Now their backs were to the wall, as one more victory by the Marlins would give them the championship.

Returning to New York for the do-or-die Game 6, the Yankees hoped that being back on their home turf would give the team a lift. But it was not to be. The Marlins started with their new twenty-three-year-old pitcher, Josh Beckett, and Beckett, pitching the game of his life, shut out the Yankees, leading the Marlins to a 2–0 victory. Shattering all expectations, the Marlins were crowned world champions. As the ecstatic Marlins players raced up to the pitcher's mound, throwing their arms around each other, the Yankee players watched with sidelong glances before retreating to their locker room. There were a lot of glum faces in that room, Matsui's among them.

Since his first at bat in Game 5, Matsui had gone twelve straight at bats without a hit. When the Yankees had won Games 2 and 3 by such convincing margins, I had thought that the series was leaning in their favor, but there had been too many missed opportunities in the subsequent games. Watching this World Series, I had thought that baseball was really a dreadful game. The baseball gods had wantonly dangled the laurel crown of victory within the Yankees' grasp, only to snatch it away.

As I was leaving Yankee Stadium, I asked a Japanese journalist I knew to deliver a message to Matsui. "Even if it's in three days or a week from now, I'll be at my hotel, and when he feels more settled, would you ask him to come see me?"

I knew that Matsui, having been entrusted with the cleanup spot, felt like he was the one most responsible for this loss. I knew that time was the only thing that would lessen his feelings of shame.

However, the very next morning, I got a call from the journalist. "Matsui wanted to know if he could come by today after he cleans out his locker."

"Is he all right? I can wait. . . ."

"He knows that you came to see the World Series, that you're busy with all of your work."

It was true, I was incredibly busy. It was the fourth time that year that I had traveled to New York, and I had accumulated enough frequent flier miles to circle the globe four times.

After he cleaned out his locker, Matsui arrived at my hotel. As usual, I was slightly nervous, but then his smiling, open face appeared in the lobby. We stood there chatting for a bit, and that night we went out for dinner. The young man who sat there with me, heartily eating his Japanese meal, hardly seemed like the player who, until the previous night, had been valiantly vying for the world championship as the New York Yankees cleanup hitter. He spoke politely, and when he occasionally told a joke, I was reminded of his state of mind just one year ago, when he had agonized over whether to move to the major leagues. I was very glad that he had joined the Yankees.

"That reminds me, earlier this year, I saw your picture in the sports column of a newspaper in Paris," I told him.

"Really, in Paris?"

"Yes, it was in the *International Herald Tribune.* It was a photo from when you were playing the Baltimore Orioles in August and you made that great play, running into the fence with a back-handed catch. Manager Torre said that a team could build a season on a play like that, didn't he?"

"I'm impressed with how much you know."

"I've turned into a fanatic about your playing."

When it was time to go, I said to him, "You can always go back to Japan with your head held high. You're the first Japanese person to hit a home run in the World Series. You are now the Yankees' pivotal batter."

"I understand. But if I could have hit better, there might be a championship ring on my finger. I still don't have enough power."

I nodded deeply and said good-bye to Matsui.

Throughout that season I had made many trips to Europe for my work. There were trips to France and Spain to see paintings, and I was following pilgrimage routes. During that time, my

biggest problem was the fact that Europeans had virtually no interest in baseball. I had no idea why Europeans were unaware of
how entertaining the sport could be. In order to find out what
happened with the Yankees and how Matsui had played, I had to
call my wife at home in Japan every day. Aside from Matsui's
record, when we spoke I would have to listen to her talk about
whether Rivera had hit a home run or if Clemens had pitched
well. My wife, the baseball authority!

But when she said, "My boy, he did it," she knew just how to
relay the details.

"Why don't they cover my boy's home run in the news in Paris?"

"Maybe they would if the batter carried a wine bottle up to bat."

Even though I couldn't get news of Matsui's play on the field, I
knew that no reporters were writing about his generous and giving spirit off the field.

IN 1998, Matsui's father, Masao, visited Vietnam, a country that
had suffered a tragic history in the twentieth century. The disrup-
tions of war went on for many years there—with the Vietnam
conflict so familiar to Americans only one phase in a longer
struggle—and as a result, there was a lot of poverty. While he was
there, Masao found out how many children there were who
wanted to go to school but could not afford it. Some of these children had been orphaned in the fighting. Masao couldn't bear to
see this. After he returned to Japan, he felt like there ought to be
something he could do for these children, so he started to send
them scholarship money. Soon Matsui joined in, becoming a sponsor to ten Vietnamese children.

When I asked him about this, it seemed like he had a great relationship with them. Here are two of the letters that these children have sent to their benefactor.

Dear Mr. Hideki Matsui,

Mr. Matsui, today is May 7, 2002. I am writing this letter to thank you, Mr. Matsui, for your support these past years. I pray for the good health of you and your whole family. The money that we received from you at the end of the school year has helped my parents even more than usual. It will also help me to prepare for the next school year. I am very grateful to you, Mr. Matsui. The beginning of May is exam period for the second semester. I have already finished seven subjects. Vietnamese, Physics, English, Chemistry, History, Geography, and Biology. Tomorrow, my last exams are in Math and Civics. I do not want to disappoint you, Mr. Matsui, so I will try to do my best on my exams. I promise to study as hard as I can so I don't disappoint you. I will pray for good health for you, Mr. Matsui.

NGUYEN AN TUONG

Mr. Matsui!

It's been three months, and now I am able to write you another letter. My name is Vo Nguyen Son Ton. I'm a ninth-grader at Le Qui Don Junior High School in Hai Duong City in Hai Duong Province. When I wrote to you three months ago, it was the middle of the school year. Now we are in the last month of school. In Vietnam, the bright red flowers are slowly turning the ground a brilliant color. That's how we know that the end of the school year is near. Right now, it's not just the end of another school year for me. I will have to say good-bye to Le Qui Don Junior High School too.

Soon I will be a high school student. There will probably be many difficulties for me to overcome. But I will not give up. Because if I fail, then I will let down my teachers and friends who are expecting me to do well. And most of all, I will disappoint you, Mr. Matsui, who I respect and who supports children like me whose parents have died. In Vietnam, the temperature rises day after day, and the sun gets stronger. What is the weather like in Japan? Someday I want to go to Japan, to see how beautiful it is there. And since I've never seen your face, I hope that I can meet my foster in person, Mr. Matsui, and we can enjoy a nice long conversation. In closing, I will pray for the health and happiness of you and your family.

SON TON

I wonder if these children know that the sponsor they've never met has traveled from Japan to America, where he is facing his greatest challenge yet in major league baseball? If they knew all that, I'm sure they would be proud of him.

Like the story that I wrote about before, the one about the girl with the congenital heart problem, there was hardly anything in the media about Matsui being a sponsor to these ten children while he was playing in Japan. Since it's a perfectly natural thing for him to do, he doesn't seem to think that it is remarkable in any way. That's his modesty. According to the Japanese way of thinking, generous deeds should be done quietly. What kind of philanthropy is Matsui practicing now that he has moved to New York? I will not ask him, nor will he speak of it. And that's just fine. Matsui believes that the Japanese way of doing things is the right way, and I'm sure he'll continue in his ways.

12

RAINING CATS AND DOGS

I n 2004, going into his second season with the Yankees, Matsui could relax a little, after the bewildering pace of the previous year. Matsui had a clear idea of the role he had played during his first year. The team expected great things in terms of powerful batting from him and the new superstar players, Alex Rodriguez and Gary Sheffield.

Believe it or not, the Yankees' opening game that year was in Tokyo, Japan, at Matsui's old stomping grounds, the Tokyo Dome. It had been forty-nine years since the Yankees had last visited Japan, back in 1955. Despite the media contingent that followed Matsui around in New York, the Yankee players were still impressed by the level of Matsui's popularity in Japan.

During interleague play that May, Matsui was in Los Angeles to play against the Dodgers. In the bus on the way to the ballpark,

Matsui received a telephone call from the team's management telling him that a young Japanese boy who had a serious illness had been admitted to a hospital in New Jersey. The boy was a huge fan of Matsui's. Matsui then called the hospital while he was still on the bus. Because the boy was suffering from a respiratory disease, Matsui was the only one who spoke during their conversation. "You mustn't let the disease win, you got it? I'll do my best if you'll do your best."

Months later, in early August, Matsui received another telephone call from management. "The boy's condition hasn't improved. Do you think you could find the time to go and visit him?"

Hearing this, Matsui replied, "I'll go there right away," and he headed for New Jersey. When he arrived at the hospital, he put on a white gown and mask and entered the boy's room. It was filled with all kinds of Hideki Matsui gear. The boy and his parents were overwhelmed to see Matsui.

Matsui sat down on the edge of the boy's bed and said, "You've got to get better. It'll be fine. You're going to be all right. Once you're well, we can play a game of catch."

The frail-bodied boy nodded vigorously at his hero, Matsui.

In that day's game against the Toronto Blue Jays, Matsui launched a three-run home run into the first level of the upper deck, and at bat in the third inning, he hit another home run. In the same inning, with the bases loaded, he hit the ball into shallow left field, bringing his total RBI for the game to six. The Yankees won 11–4.

Matsui had heard the story of Babe Ruth's famous promise to a boy on his sickbed. "I thought it might make this boy feel better if I promised him I'd hit a home run," he said. "So I did that for the boy, because when someone is trying to recover, you can't forget what other people's power and energy can do. That's why I have to try so hard in every game."

I visited Yankee Stadium ten times in 2003 and 2004. I also made it to Toronto, Canada, and Boston for the postseason, and to Miami for the World Series. During those games, I loved seeing all the fans wearing Matsui's number, but I especially loved to see all the young boys and girls who looked up to him and followed his career so closely. A lot of those kids seemed to have one thing in common—they appeared to be shy, modest kids who appreciated Matsui's quiet, dignified style, so at odds with the brash and often arrogant ways of other baseball superstars.

Matsui has many young fans in Japan as well. Twelve years earlier, when Matsui had begun his career with the Giants, he had stated his number one goal as a professional player: "I want to be the kind of player who kids come to the ballpark to see play."

In that, he has been successful beyond his wildest dreams. Matsui really does love kids. I think he wants to feed the dreams of children, who still have their futures before them. He has had a kind and gentle nature ever since he was a boy himself.

In Japan there is a holiday known as "Tanabata," or "Seven Evenings," which comes on July 7 (the seventh day of the seventh month). It is also called the Star Festival because the constellations Hikoboshi and Orihime, representing two star-crossed lovers, are only allowed to meet on this one day in the entire year, and we celebrate the holiday by hanging decorations on bamboo branches. It's sort of like the Japanese version of a Christmas tree, except Christmas in the West comes in the winter, while Tanabata falls during our rainy season.

One Tanabata when Matsui was eight, it was raining as usual, which meant that there would be no baseball after school. Young Matsui was on his way home, walking past rice paddies and farmland, when he heard something over the sound of the rain. A faint voice. When he stood still and listened more closely, he realized that he was hearing the thin meows of a kitten. Matsui tried to find where the sound was coming from. Was it from a ridge in the rice paddy? Or from the gutter? He ran all around, but he couldn't find the kitten. Then he noticed a farmer's barn. He rushed inside. There, underneath a tractor, was a tiny black-and-white cat, drenched from the rain and shivering. Matsui nestled the kitten against his chest. It was so small that it fit in his hand, and so thin it was just fur and bones. *It's going to die,* he thought to himself. Matsui put the kitten inside his shirt and took it home. "Dad, Mom, we have to save this kitten, right? Can we keep her? Otherwise she'll die."

"Okay," they said, giving in.

The kitten was completely covered in mud. She couldn't open her eyes; she couldn't even drink milk. The Matsuis took her to the veterinarian.

When they got back home, Matsui made a bed for the kitten and asked his father, "What should we name her?"

His advice was, "Since you brought her home on the seventh day of the seventh month, why not name her Nana?" ("Nana" is the Japanese word for the number seven.)

With Matsui's devoted nursing, little by little Nana grew stronger, and soon she could open her eyes. *What beautiful eyes,* Matsui thought. He wondered why it was that he had his parents, and Nana didn't have any parents. *That means I've got to be her dad.*

Nana lived a long life of eighteen years with Matsui. When I heard this story, I understood why Matsui loves children and animals so much.

I think I have mentioned that the only thing in our house signed by Matsui is a photograph inscribed to Ice, aka the Philosopher, our hard-to-please dog. Hiroko and I had a bit of a quarrel when we first got that dog.

My wife had actually wanted to have a dog ever since she found a cat who had given birth to three kittens under our house. My wife discovered them and started giving them milk. The kittens were very watchful, and they didn't take to my wife at all. She patiently continued to give them milk until, one day, the mother cat took her kittens off somewhere. My wife took it personally. She moped around the house in a bad mood, brooding.

"Why don't we get a cat?" I suggested. She had said those three kittens were so cute.

So Hiroko went to a pet store. But while she was there, she fell in love at first sight with a puppy who looked very unhappy. Meanwhile, I was about to leave on a research trip to Europe.

"Would it be okay to get a dog?" my wife asked before I left.

"What? A dog? What about last time?"

She had told me about having once had a dog in Tokyo, a neurotic, overbred animal who had made her life miserable.

"But that was when I was an actress and I was never at home," she protested. "I was young then, not ready for the responsibility. I think it would be fine now."

I was still worried. "If you really want to get a dog, I don't mind, but we should think the decision through logically. After all, a dog's life span is shorter than a human's. The dog will probably die before we do. No matter how well you take care of him, he won't live beyond fifteen or twenty years at most. How old will you be then? Will you be able to deal with the dog's death? I'm just worried about you," I said.

"I'll think about it," she said.

"We'll talk more when I get back," I said and left for Europe.

After several days on my trip, I arrived at my hotel in Paris and phoned home to Japan.

"You have to think of a name soon."

"A name for what?"

"For our pet dog." That was Hiroko's way of cheerfully telling me we now had a pet.

When I returned home from my monthlong trip, I saw that the refrigerator, usually stocked with beef jerky and smoked fish to go with my whiskey, was now stacked with dog food. And in my study, a favorite side bench was gone, replaced by the dog's bed.

At first I was a bit resentful, but the puppy was as sweet as an angel, and I couldn't resist for long. I named him Ice, and merely staring at him soon became the central activity in our house. I would watch Matsui's games on TV with Hiroko and the dog, and whenever Matsui hit a home run, my wife would jump up and clap her hands together. Seeing her excitement, Ice would jump up too and start barking.

At my wife's bidding, on a trip to Manhattan I went to a sporting goods shop and bought a pinstripe outfit and a Yankees cap especially made for dogs (who in the world makes such things?). Although for Ice, it would have been more appropriate to wear a Cossack hat. The dog's sulkiness could only be compared to Tolstoy's melancholy.

When my wife spoke to Matsui on the phone, he would often ask, "How is Ice doing?" This always made her happy. I noticed that Matsui also seemed to have a certain way with my hard-to-please wife.

MATSUI continued to play well during the 2004 season, establishing himself as the Yankee left fielder. At one point, I met Matsui's mother and older brother, Toshiki, at Yankee Stadium.

His brother, an architect, seemed like a kind man. When I saw Matsui a few days later, I said to him, "You have a nice brother."

"He's the greatest," he replied happily. "The reason I'm playing baseball like this is all because of him."

A new Matsui commemorative stadium that had opened in Matsui's hometown that year had been designed by Toshiki. As I heard Matsui talk about his brother, I thought that it might be nice for Ice to have a brother as well. I decided that having two dogs would be even better than having one. I called my wife from New York and asked her what she thought about getting another dog. She said that her hands were full just taking care of Ice, but I cajoled her into looking for another dog.

The next afternoon, Hiroko called me back. "I looked all over," she said.

"And?"

"There weren't any cute dogs."

"Keep looking," I said.

When I called home again three days later, she still hadn't found one.

Five days later: "There's a dog with a crumpled-up face who

they haven't been able to sell. He doesn't seem to have a very good temperament. The amount on his price tag keeps going down."

"That one sounds good," I told her. "Bring that dog home."

When I got back from my trip, the new dog was there. However, Ice didn't seem too pleased to have a brother. All the puppy had to do was come near him, and he would growl and menace him. "Be nice to each other," Hiroko would say, but Ice would just look the other way.

I watched Ice's behavior and said to him, "You may think you're a Socratic philosopher, but really you're more of a Sophist. I'm disappointed in you."

IN October of that year, Matsui hit his thirty-first home run of the season at Yankee Stadium. The Yankees went into the playoffs as the Eastern Division champions for the seventh year in a row. The postseason began the same way as the previous year—the Yankees played the Twins in the divisional series, beating them 3–1, and again faced the Red Sox in the American League Championship Series.

Going into the series, the Red Sox were favored, but the Yankees won the first three games in a row. Matsui was in top form with two home runs in Game 3, but in Game 4, even with the Yankees in the lead and the ace reliever Mariano Rivera pitching, the Red Sox scored an upset in extra innings. Game 5 also went into extra innings, and the Yankees lost again. Riding their momentum, the Red Sox won four straight games, dashing the Yankees' dream of the world championship. In the seven games of the ALCS, Matsui's batting average was .412; he had ten hits, nine of which were extra base hits. His power hitting tied the American League postseason record. Yet these personal triumphs were bittersweet, only underscoring Matsui's appreciation for how harsh the path to a major-league world championship could be.

That year, when I was away on another long trip, there was an earthquake near where we lived, big enough that one of the buildings at an old elementary school collapsed. Fortunately no one died, but many people's homes were destroyed. My wife brought blankets and water to the devastated areas. When I heard about all this on an overseas telephone call and pictured my wife doing what she could to help the victims, I suddenly realized that this instinct for philanthropy was one of the reasons that she and Matsui got along so well.

After the loss to the Red Sox, Matsui returned to Japan in good standing. The day of the annual dinner with Matsui and my wife was approaching. Since we would be meeting in Tokyo, I went ahead and spent the night before the dinner in the city. The following day I got a call from Hiroko.

She told me that our new little dog had Parvovirus. "This morning, he vomited up an awful lot of blood. Right now they're keeping him at the vet's."

I asked her to wait while I called a veterinarian I knew.

"Parvovirus is very serious," the vet told me. "There's a ninety-five percent fatality rate."

"What should we do?" I asked my veterinary friend.

"There's a doctor I know in your town. Bring the dog to his hospital. There have been cases where dogs have recovered after receiving human medicine."

I called Hiroko back. "My friend says this virus is very serious.

We can reschedule with Matsui anytime, and there's always next year. You have to take the dog to the hospital right away."

It was a shame to have to cancel her dinner that she had been so looking forward to, but it pained me to think about our beloved little dog's body being attacked by such a malevolent virus. When I met up with Matsui later, I explained the situation to him. He wanted to call my wife. After a while on the phone, he said that my wife wanted to speak to me.

"What's the matter?" I said.

"I don't know, suddenly she just fell silent," Matsui said.

"What did you say to her?"

"I told her that I would pray to God for the dog's recovery," Matsui replied.

I took the receiver. I could hear my wife on the other end, sobbing.

"What's wrong?" Matsui asked me with concern.

"What you said was so kind that it made her cry," I told him.

My wife, despite her kind nature, was not easily brought to tears. My wife, who was normally about as sentimental a woman as Margaret Thatcher, was crying. Once again I wondered what kind of young man Matsui was.

I don't know if God heard his prayers, but our little dog survived.

After that, Hiroko would say to the dog, "My boy prayed for you, and you came back from heaven. So you had better behave, or Matsui will scold you for me."

We named the dog Nobo. (At first, we had tried to give him the name, Kees, like the Yan-*kees,* but we had to change it because whenever my wife would call out the name "Kees," the other dog, Ice, would also come running. So I decided to rename him after one of my favorite poets, Shiki Masaoka, who was the first in Japan to write poems and haiku about baseball—he was called "Noboru" by those who knew him.) Whenever Nobo was being mischievous, my wife would tell him that Matsui was going to scold him, and he would stare back at her blankly. I wondered if his older brother, who hadn't met Matsui either, knew what she was talking about.

The new year approached, and Matsui left Tokyo and returned to his hometown. This was when the Indian Ocean tsunami occurred off the coast of Sumatra, causing a tragic loss of life. The next day, my wife sent a donation to the Red Cross. That night, we saw on the TV news that Matsui had donated ¥50 million (approximately $450,000) to the victims. My wife applauded at the television. I regretted that I had thought it was a good idea to quit baseball forty years earlier.

13

THE SPIRIT
OF THE YANKEES

If you watch baseball over a long time, there are things that you see that you will probably never forget. Plays that demonstrate amazing athletic ability or courage. They're a testament to how dramatic a sport the game of baseball can be.

Whenever I see a play like that, I always murmur to myself, *There must be a god of baseball.* At this point I have written several novels that use baseball as a backdrop. Among those, I was lucky enough that one of them won a very prestigious literary award in Japan, and from then on I was considered a professional writer.

On July 1, 2004, I saw such a play on television. The location was Yankee Stadium. The Red Sox were up, and the Yankees were on defense. Tanyon Sturtze pitched to Trot Nixon, who hit a foul fly ball toward third base near the left-field stands. Jeter, the shortstop, went after the ball. As he was running for it, he realized that the ball was about to go into the stands, but at the same time, he could not stop his momentum. Jeter caught the ball in fair territory and then went diving headfirst into the stands. For a moment, you couldn't even see his upper body; all you could see were his long legs sticking out like posts. The fans rushed to try to lift Jeter up in their arms. The look on their faces said, *He's injured, it's serious.*

After being lifted up by a member of the ballpark staff, Jeter reappeared with his face spattered with fresh blood. He had persevered without regard for injury or anything else, and he would have regretted it if he hadn't caught the ball. The seats in Yankee Stadium are made from solid steel. And he had leapt right into them, face first. Manager Torre ran right over. Whenever there was an accident on the field with a Yankee player, Torre was the first one to jump off the bench, always so swift it was hard to believe, especially compared to his pace when he went out to advise about changing a pitcher. When Jeter was led back to the dugout, with blood running down his face, a round of applause went up from the stands. It came out later that when Jeter was on his way to the hospital, he said that he would soon be back to play. The eleventh captain of the Yankees, Jeter knew what a baseball player ought to do. He knew what it meant to play and to do your best in the name of victory. He knew why the Yankees had won so many times over their long history in the major leagues. In other words, the timeless Yankee spirit lives on in the heart of a genuine player like Derek Jeter. In all of the Yankees' history, I don't know if there is a player with more guts.

On May 11, 2006, Matsui ran to get to a shallow line drive that Mark Loretta of the Red Sox hit into left field. It was a catch Matsui should have made easily, sliding into it with his glove extended toward the ball. *I will catch that ball. I won't let it be a hit.* This was clearly what Matsui was thinking as he went to make the play. But the smooth grass of left field was slightly damp from rain, and as Matsui held out his glove, it turned dramatically in the opposite direction, fracturing his wrist. This put an end to Matsui's consecutive game streak, which had continued from when he had been playing in Japan, resulting in his first and painful long-term rest from playing baseball in more than twenty years. But what received the most attention wasn't the fact that he sustained an injury or snapped his streak. What impressed those of us who are baseball fans was that, with his left wrist broken, he still got the ball in his glove and, crawling on the grass, managed to throw the ball in with his right hand. As I watched this in amazement, I realized that it epitomized how valuable Matsui is as a player. As long as the ball was still in play, he would try his best to do what was expected of him. He was a professional ballplayer, with the spirit of the Yankees in him, the same spirit that inspired Derek Jeter. In these two plays, I saw the dignity of baseball. And such wonderful young men.

And so it comes as no surprise that these two guys would respect each other and become close friends. They can appreciate each other.

I once asked Matsui about the time when Jeter dove into the stands.

He shook his head admiringly. "I think he's an amazing player. The team couldn't lose the game after that. When we heard that he had been taken to the hospital, it was like the rest of the team

was going to play their best for him, like they learned the impor-
tance of not giving up. He's a real Yankee."

Matsui must have been born under a lucky star. When he
joined the Yankees, he was fortunate enough to come to know
Manager Torre. I don't know if Matsui would be the same player
if it weren't for Torre. The player that Torre wants Matsui to be
and the player that Matsui wants to become are one and the same.
I write it over and over: The beauty of baseball is that it is a game
in which everyone does their best for the sake of winning. The
players who understand that are impressive. More than a glorious
personal record, or a brilliant play, all of the charm of the game
can be found when the team comes together to win. It's like the
most important spiritual quality of a life well-lived.

That mental capacity—to not give up, to withstand difficult
challenges—brings everyone together in order to achieve something special and enduring. As far as Matsui was concerned, he
was certainly indebted to Torre as the greatest mentor he could
have imagined for his introduction to the major leagues.

Bernie Williams, Jason Giambi, Jorge Posada, Robin Ventura . . .
The list of nice guys who helped support Matsui goes on and on.
But among his teammates, I'm sure Matsui counts on Derek Jeter
the most. Perhaps one of the reasons why is that they are both the
same age and they are both single.

For the Yankees, the 2005 season proved to be a string of difficult games. Part of it was that the pitchers weren't performing as
everyone had expected in the spring, and on top of that the team
seemed to be missing something. Nobody was more aware of that
than their captain, Derek Jeter. It seemed that Matsui was ex-

tremely tuned in to how Jeter was feeling. The fact that, in Japan, Matsui had been captain of the Giants may have had something to do with it.

In 2005, the Yankees lost the division playoff series to the Los Angeles Angels of Anaheim. After their loss, the Yankee players were scheduled to take off from Anaheim to return to New York at one o'clock in the morning. The flight was late, leaving at 3:00 A.M., and they had to stop and refuel in Houston—it sounded like it was a terrible trip. The plane was carrying a team of guys who had played hard all year, only to lose. . . . The story I'm about to tell you is a conversation between the normally reserved Matsui and a Japanese journalist, Musashi Asada, who was based in New York. Although the journalist is young, he is a talented writer. I think it's a really great story.

In their final game against the Angels, Matsui was the last batter up. Looking for two runs and with two outs in the ninth inning, there were two men on base. With a long hit, they could tie it up. With a home run, they could turn it around. Matsui hit a hard ground ball that headed between first and second base. The Angels' first baseman was Darin Erstad, a well-regarded defensive player. Erstad dove toward the ball. The ball settled into the outstretched glove of the left-handed Erstad. Matsui ran as hard as he could, but the season ended on a play that was as close as a hairsbreadth.

After the game, Matsui apologized to Torre. I'm sorry for not getting the hit. Torre said, Not at all, that's not it at all, Hideki. He told him that it wasn't his fault. Torre's words seemed heartfelt. He also said that, in all his years as a player and a manager, he had never seen a player apologize and take responsibility for the team's loss.

But Matsui honestly felt responsible and really wanted to bring those runners home. In Japan, it's very common after a game to search out the cause of a loss and to give names of specific players, so it's not at all unusual for a player to assume responsibility. In any case, Matsui felt remorseful as he flew home. Some of the players on the plane tried their best to act cheerful, some of them were even playing cards, but the mood on the plane was decidedly heavy.

Matsui got up to go to the bathroom. The last seat on the plane was always reserved as Jeter's seat. When Matsui tried to walk past him, Jeter called out, "Matsu."

Then he said, "You are my favorite player."

Matsui thought he was joking, as he often did, so he replied, "I don't think so." But then his expression became very serious. He said, "Jee, you are my favorite player."

Next Jeter asked him, "Matsu, what are you going to do now?" Jeter must have been concerned about what Matsui's plans were. He knew that Matsui's three-year contract with the Yankees was ending that year.

"I don't know yet. How many years do you have left, Jee?"

"I've got five years to go. . . ."

"Well then, maybe I'll sign a five-year contract, too. . . ."

"Really, Matsu? Then after five years, we can go play together in Japan." This conversation was half in jest, but I like to think about it as a pleasant talk between two teammates. It appeared that both players still had plenty of enthusiasm left in them as members of the Yankees.

Reminiscing about the 2005 season, Matsui also had this to say about Jeter.

"It was spectacular to watch Jeter play from the last game of the regular season through the end of the playoffs. He had a lot of hits, especially when the team seemed like they were losing their fighting spirit.

"My trust in him has grown even stronger. I have really come to understand Jeter as a player. Of course, he pulls his own weight on the team, but he's the kind of guy who just stands firm. Even when he's completely physically exhausted, he holds out until the end. He's Mister Yankee."

Matsui heaped praise upon his close friend.

"Whether or not he's hitting, his attitude doesn't change one bit. He always puts the team ahead of himself. And he has such a clear awareness of exactly how he influences the team."

Matsui had made a good friend in Jeter. Someday these two . . . no, this season even, I hope to see their smiling faces covered in confetti from a victory parade in Manhattan.[1]

14

FROM BATTLEFIELD
TO BASEBALL FIELD

On May 3, 2006, my wife and I were in Poland. Hiroko had always wanted to visit what was left of the concentration camp at Auschwitz. She had been to the atomic bomb memorial museums in Hiroshima and Nagasaki, and she had told me that, if we ever had the chance to go, she would like to learn more about the war in Europe. I think that she wanted to bring Matsui along to visit the concentration camp, and she thought that she would first go to see it for herself. This trip had several purposes. One of them was that, five years earlier, my wife's father had passed away, and last year her mother had also died. When each of them had been battling their illnesses, Hiroko had made a pilgrimage for her parents to the Black Madonna of Montserrat in Spain. As a result of this, we believe that her parents both lived far longer than the doctors' prognoses. On this trip, we had come to offer our thanks to the Virgin Mary. After that, we would travel to Poland, and then afterward we would cross the Atlantic Ocean to see Matsui play at Yankee Stadium. I think Hiroko was looking forward to that more than anything. But unfortunately we had to cancel that part of the trip after Matsui's injury, and our trip ended up being confined to Europe.

To be honest, I had a hard time understanding the way that my wife and Matsui were always thinking about other people, wanting to do things like visit Mother Teresa's house or Auschwitz. Since the summer when I was five years old, all I ever wanted to do was play, and I hadn't really matured much since; I had only grown into an adult who had learned the art of cleverly concealing the fact that he was having fun.

"Why do people make war? Why do they do such a foolish thing?" Whenever Hiroko would ask me this, I would find myself at a loss.

In the town where I was born, there were monuments dedicated to the souls of those who had died in World War II. When I was a child, during the summer Bon festival, there were many mothers who came to pray for sons who had gone to the front with the army and who had not returned. They would keep a lamp lit in front of their houses and wait all night to make it easy for their beloved sons to find their way home. It was the same for those who were in the air raids. On the day that Matsui arrived in New York, he went to Ground Zero, where he stood motionlessly and prayed for an hour in a snowstorm.

There were many major-league players who fought on the battlefields of World War II. The winningest left-handed pitcher in history, Warren Spahn, fought against the German army on the front lines in Europe, and the famous Yankee catcher Yogi Berra was part of the continental tactical operations off the coast of Normandy. When the Cleveland Indians' Bob Feller, who had joined the major leagues at seventeen and had twenty wins in only three years, heard about the attack on Pearl Harbor in December 1941, he enlisted in the Navy two days later, joining the combat on the battleship *Alabama.* It was the same with the Yankees' Jerry Coleman. This was at a very critical point in these athletes' playing careers, but in order to serve their country, they put patriotism before baseball. I have heard there were 1,100 major-league players who served in World War II. Sadly two of them died in action, Elmore Gedeon and Harry O'Neill. Gedeon died in France, and O'Neill was killed in action at Iwo Jima.

There were sixty-nine professional baseball players in Japan who served in the military and died in action. Among them, some were part of a special attack corps that flew sorties from battleships. The famous pitcher Eiji Sawamura, who had played against the visiting all-star players from the major leagues before the war and had racked up strikeouts against Babe Ruth and Lou Gehrig, died in the war. And many more Americans and Japanese who loved baseball died on the battlefield.

During World War II, the battle between America and Japan began when Japan attacked Pearl Harbor without a declaration of war. I don't think Americans will ever forget Pearl Harbor. Nowadays, most Japanese people may have forgotten what happened after the war. The occupation forces, composed mainly of the American military, occupied Japan and poured an abundance of energy into our country to reconstruct it. Today, most young people in Japan probably don't even realize the tragic fate we escaped.

They may not have any idea how cruel war can be. At my age, I have memories of the war, since my hometown was near Hiroshima, and I have participated in demonstrations for a ban on nuclear weapons. I know the misery that war brings. In elementary school, I drank skim milk from America in order to grow up big and strong. But the thing for which I am most grateful is having had the peace to play baseball. For almost fifteen years, all I did was play the game. I had the most wonderful time, and I am proud of all the friends that I made. Now, as an adult, when I encounter difficulties, I compare them to the game's crucial moments and convince myself that I am capable of overcoming whatever they are. When I was a boy, all over Japan kids would play baseball in any vacant lot. There are many things to learn from baseball, one of which is how a single Japanese major-league player is able to communicate with people from a different country due to the cross-cultural appeal of the game. I give thanks for this sport and am also grateful for the Americans who created, shaped, and upheld the traditions of the game. As long as Matsui and Ichiro are playing in America, I believe that our future can be a bright one where people of all cultures work together as a team and where teammates will not hate each other or point guns at each other.

People who gain power eventually want to use it. If a country is powerful, they build a military to display their might. That is how countries are, how men are. Modesty is one important virtue that can stop the abuse of power. I have seen such modesty in Matsui and believe that as long as he is playing baseball in the major leagues, there is something important to be learned on the field.

15

"YANKEES FANS ARE SUCH WONDERFUL PEOPLE!"

Breaking his left wrist was the first significant injury of Matsui's professional baseball career. For that matter, it was the first injury that had ever interfered with his ability to play baseball. Even during his rambunctious boyhood, he had never gotten hurt running through the fields or playing on the beach. The clear evidence of this was his consecutive streak of 1,768 games, continuing from his play in Japan, that was now at an end. The truth was that, in the twelve years since he had turned pro, Matsui hadn't had any injuries . . . until now. I wanted to try to contact Matsui as soon as I heard the news, but I decided to wait.

If I had spoken to him, I would have told him to take his time and concentrate on recovering at his own pace, but I was sure that Matsui already knew that. I was quite familiar with his sense of responsibility.

But this was the first time Matsui had encountered a physical impediment to his formidable willpower. How would he handle it? I could only imagine how frustrating it must be. Nevertheless, I found myself hoping that this adversity would improve Matsui, not just as a baseball player but as an individual as well. After all, almost every famous baseball player has faced difficult times. When someone comes face-to-face with challenges and manages to overcome them, they grow as a person. I knew it would be painful for Matsui, but I had the feeling that by conquering these circumstances, a new Matsui would emerge. My wife and both of the dogs prayed for Matsui's speedy and complete recovery. In Japan, the number of Yankees games that were televised decreased dramatically once Matsui was absent from the lineup. This was very sad for me, because I'd become a real Yankees fan. I still enjoyed watching the Yankees games even without Matsui. I liked to watch Derek Jeter and Mariano Rivera, and I was always happy when the Yankees won. But all the same, Matsui's absence from the field only made me more aware than ever of how large a presence he was in my life.

The day after his injury, Matsui released a statement. "Due to this injury," the statement read, "I feel very sorry and, at the same time, very disappointed to have let my teammates down."

The American media was surprised by his comments. Few players had ever apologized for an injury that had occurred accidentally during a game. After all, it wasn't Matsui's fault! But the statement was praised as further testament to Matsui's character and dignity. It was also classic Yankees style. Everyone now eagerly awaited Matsui's speedy return.

The first half of the 2006 season ended. The Yankees were having a tough time. Matsui wasn't the only player on the disabled list. Gary Sheffield, another of the team's big hitters, was also out. And as if that didn't put them at enough of a disadvantage, their pitching staff was unsettled too.

In Japan, the month or so known as the rainy season ends in July, and that's when summer begins in earnest. The Japanese sports media began to focus on Matsui's comeback. Articles appeared every day in the sports pages about his recovery, speculating that Matsui would probably return to the lineup in August.

"Won't you be going to New York soon to check up on how my boy is doing?" Hiroko asked me one day after the Japanese television broadcast of a Yankees game had ended.

"I'm sure there will be an announcement when he's made a full recovery," I replied. "I'll wait until then."

The truth was that I hadn't had any contact with Matsui since his injury. Even if I had gone to visit him, there wasn't anything I could have done, and I knew it was most important for him to concentrate on his recovery.

Finally, in August, four months after his injury, Matsui put his uniform back on and started training to play again. He began his rehab in the minors, playing for the Class AA Trenton Thunder. Meanwhile, I prepared to make the trip to see his return to the major leagues. My plan was to be in New York by September 10. I would travel by way of Paris and London, with a side trip to Scotland, where I needed to do some research for a new novel. However, on the afternoon of my departure from Japan, there was a newsflash on television announcing the discovery of an attempted terrorist plot in London. When I called my travel agent's office, they said there was mass confusion in London. My trip was canceled. As more information about the plot became known, I was amazed and frightened by the extent of the terrorists' plans to blow up airplanes over the Atlantic Ocean.

Matsui's return was set for September 12, 2006, when the Yankees would face the Tampa Bay Devil Rays at Yankee Stadium.

On the morning of the thirteenth, thanks to the time difference with New York, Hiroko, Ice, Nobo, and I were installed in front of the television.

My wife turned to me. "This reminds me of another morning, four years ago, when we were sitting here like this, waiting for my boy."

"You're right," I said. "But now our household has one more member."

As I watched the TV, I thought about what the past three and a half years had been like for Matsui, playing for the Yankees. I was looking forward to seeing him, of course, but I knew that Matsui had yet to have the kind of fantastic season that he had hoped for when he first arrived in New York. Nevertheless, in his first three years, Matsui had certainly become a member of the Yankees team, and I knew that was no small achievement. But Matsui had not yet displayed his full talent either. I knew he had more in him.

There was Matsui's face on the television screen. At last, he appeared on the field. Wearing his pinstripes, Matsui jogged onto the outfield. I could almost feel the buzz in Yankee Stadium. *Yes, that's just how Matsui should look,* I thought. They began announcing the starting players' lineup, displaying their names on the center field scoreboard. When the announcer read, "Number 55, Hideki Matsui," a cheer went up in Yankee Stadium.

"Wow, it seems like more people than usual are clapping," Hiroko said. "My boy must really be popular."

I had to agree.

Twenty minutes into the game, something happened that neither my wife nor I could have imagined. After the Devil Rays' first at bat, the Yankees came up. Their batting lineup was on fire from the start, with Bobby Abreu, batting in the fifth position, hitting a three-run home run. After the next two batters, with one out and men on first and third, Matsui came to the plate. As he slowly made his way to the batter's box, a roar swept through Yankee Stadium. Every fan in the stands stood up and turned toward Matsui.

The applause did not die down as Matsui came up to bat, and he took off his helmet and saluted the fans. In response, the entire ballpark clapped and cheered even more. The announcer said, "All of these fans are very happy to see Matsui return. And it's the best situation for Matsui."

"Yankees fans are such wonderful people," Hiroko said, her eyes welling up.

I felt the same way. What an amazing team, and what amazing fans. At that moment, as my heart swelled with pride, it seemed to me that Yankees fans must be the most passionate fans in the whole world.

My feelings were quite different from how I had felt that spring four years earlier when, in his first game at Yankee Stadium, Matsui had hit a grand slam. What had surged through me then had been the pure joy that a baseball lover feels when he sees a never-to-be-forgotten play. But now, seeing all the fans on their feet, I realized just how much Matsui had accomplished as a Yankee during the past four years.

Baseball is such a wonderful sport.

Matsui had a gift in return for the fans' impressive reception. In his first at bat, he stroked a hit to shallow center field. But that wasn't the end of it. He had base hits in his second, third, and fourth at bats as well. It was as if all his pent-up frustration from those months when he hadn't been able to play exploded at the plate that night.

Watching Matsui reach base in his fourth at bat, even Jeter appeared to be astounded. The look on his face seemed to say, "Man, he's some kind of player!"

That night, Matsui received two separate standing ovations as he stood on first base.

In the off-season, Matsui reminisced about his return game. "I was really pleased," he said. "I never imagined anything like that would happen when I returned to the lineup. But the applause and the cheers melted away all the pain and struggle of those four long months of rehabilitation."

Hiroko, who was now in the highest of spirits, gave our two dogs a rather large piece of meat for dinner that night, and the two of us indulged in fancier-than-usual champagne. The next day, the newspapers in New York and Japan were covered with the names Hideki Matsui and Godzilla.

"I guess Matsui's back," I said.

I reserved my ticket to travel to New York on the day that the Yankees won the American League Eastern division. In the divisional series playoff that began on October 3, 2006, the Yankees won Game 1 against the Detroit Tigers 8–4. After their spirited attack in that game, anyone could have been forgiven for assuming that the Yankees would crush the Tigers and go on to win the World Series. But, with the baseball gods in mind, I was glad that I would be arriving in time for Game 2.

It had been a long time since I had seen Matsui play in person, and I was especially looking forward to seeing him now, when he seemed to be playing near the peak of his abilities. However, the Yankees' offense sputtered in Game 2, leaving lots of runners on base. Although Matsui had two base hits, the Bronx Bombers lost 4–3. At that point, the series moved to Detroit. But because I was confident in the Yankees' ultimate victory, I decided to wait for the series to return to New York rather than follow the team to Detroit. That proved to be a mistake. In Game 3, Kenny Rogers, the Tigers' pitcher, hurled a shutout against the Yankees' lineup, and the Tigers' batters were on fire, powering the team to a 6–0 victory. In the critical Game 4, the Tigers' starting pitcher, Jeremy Bonderman, provided another dominating performance, and the Yankees lost again 8–3. To everyone's surprise, the Yankees were eliminated from the postseason. Somewhere, the baseball gods were laughing.

Several days later, I met with Matsui, and we had a meal together.

"What a shame," I said to him.

"Yes, that's baseball for you," he replied.

We ate together quietly that night.

"Has your wrist fully healed?" I asked.

Matsui smiled, showing his white teeth. "It's still a little uncomfortable. Like the doctor said in his diagnosis, it will take six months for a complete recovery, so there's still some time to go."

As I listened to what he said, I thought to myself, *That's right, it's not even half a year since he broke it.* That made his performance after returning to the lineup all the more extraordinary.

Watching Matsui sipping his tea, I realized that this was the fourth year in a row the two of us had gone out to eat together after the Yankees' season had ended. I contemplated how many of Matsui's fans, how my family, and even I myself had been inspired by his courage over those years. No matter what, he always gave his all. Anyone who had ever seen him play knew that. To watch Matsui in action was to understand just how much this young man poured into each game.

The young man whom I had first met ten years earlier had matured into a fine adult. It was like a sapling growing into a tall tree, the way that it is hard to notice how each month its trunk grows wider and its branches grow longer, until suddenly one day you look and the sapling is gone, and a strong and massive tree stands in its place.

Hideki Matsui had certainly grown larger, but I don't think he's finished yet. I wonder what kind of player he still hopes to become, what his goals are now. Will it be next season that the tree bursts into its full flowering? I hope so, and I look forward to the day when people will gather in its shade to gaze upon the beautiful, modest flowers blooming there.

1 6

MATSUI IN THE SPRING

As spring approaches in 2007, my family and I are watching our garden as the snow begins to melt. A young seedling is shaking off winter's snowy coat and stretching its limbs toward the sky. In Tampa, Florida, the Yankees have begun spring training. Every day brings fresh news about Matsui.

Last fall, several days after Matsui's impressive return to the game in Yankee Stadium, Hiroko consulted with our gardener and decided to plant a tree in our garden that is native to the New York area. The gardener suggested an oak. We were all there to greet him when he arrived with the seedling in his truck. The dogs seemed to think that the gardener was there to play with them as he dug up the earth.

"Hey, you two, leave him alone while he's working," I said.

But the dogs continued to run around the tree that, a few hours later, my wife decided to name Hideki.

After the tree was planted, Hiroko said to the dogs, "This tree's name is Hideki. Don't even think about peeing or doing any of your business under this tree."

They just looked back at my wife, who was in high spirits, and got back to their jumping around.

Later, at Christmastime, she hung lights in a heart shape from the branches of "Hideki" and decorated it with Yankee figurines and Christmas ornaments. Spring will soon be in full bloom. For my family, this spring means that Hideki is now in our garden as well as on the baseball field. Springtime, when the baseball season begins, is our favorite time of year.

One afternoon, Hiroko and I were standing, with the older philosopher dog, Ice, and his younger, wilder brother, Nobo, all of us under Hideki's tree.

An east wind had blown away the snow clouds, and the branches on Hideki's seedling with their new buds stretched toward the expansive blue sky. This tree will have to wait for the warm summer sunlight, and then it will have to weather the heavy snow of winter on its own. Yet someday it will be covered in new leaves, and then in the autumn, we will be able to admire its beautiful foliage. Of course, this tree will never be able to communicate with us in words, but it will set its roots firmly in the ground and go about doing what it needs to do to survive. It is a humble living thing. Someday when it grows tall, we will look up at this tree and offer words of gratitude.

"I wonder how well my boy will do this year?" Hiroko asked.

Ever since Matsui had returned to Japan in November, he had been more focused than ever on his training. Journalists who had observed Matsui had commented on the "ferocity" of his approach.

"I think he will play better this year than last year," I told Hiroko. "And next year even more so."

The dogs barked at our feet. I could see the telltale white butterflies that signal spring's arrival in the garden.

"Well, you both ought to pray for Matsui," she said to the dogs. "If you root with all your hearts for him, then maybe you'll get some steak for dinner."

As we turned to head back into the house, I heard the gentle sound of leaves rustling in the breeze behind us.

ENDNOTES

1. A CHILD OF BASEBALL

1. Jack Curry, "Matsui's Hello: One Colossal Grand Slam," *The New York Times,* April 9, 2003.

2. THE STAR, MODESTY INCLUDED

1. Bill Madden and Christian Red, "Boss Brushes Back Hideki, Weaver Makes Pitch for Contreras, Better Bats," *New York Daily News,* May 27, 2003.

2. Ibid.

3. Gaku Tashiro, Anthony McCarron, Dan Graziano, and Don Amore, *Hideki Matsui's Spirit* (Tokyo: Fusosha, 2003), 27.

4. Ibid.

8. "Postwar Japan Sends Its Finest Citizens to America"

1. Shizuka Ijuin, "Postwar Japan Sends Its Finest Citizens to America," *Shukan Bunshun,* November 14, 2002.

9. War, Peace, and Ground Zero

1. Hideki Matsui Kanagawa Prefecture Conference for the Promotion and Advancement of Human Rights, *A Precious Gift: An Anthology of Messages, 3rd Edition* (Kanagawa, Japan: Center for Human Rights Affairs, 1999).

10. The Mentors Behind Matsui

1. Tomoshige Yamashita and Shigenori Matsushita, *If You Change Your Mind: The Man Who Made Hideki Matsui* (Tokyo: Asahi Shimbun, 2003).

13. The Spirit of the Yankees

1. Musashi Asada, "Hideki Matsui," *Nihon Keizai Shimbun,* 2005.

ACKNOWLEDGMENTS

I would like to thank Hideki Matsui for his utmost cooperation, and Masao and Satoko Matsui for providing such valuable photographs.

I would like to express my gratitude to Allison Markin Powell, without whom this book would not have reached American readers; my editor at Random House, Jennifer Osborne, and Kay Ohara at Random House Kodansha, for their professional advice; and my U.S. agent, Farley Chase, at Waxman Literary Agency. I would also like to thank Akihiro Miyata at Random House Kodansha, who has supported my writing career in Japan for a long time, and my office staff for their daily administrative support.

Lastly, I'd like to send a thank you to my wife and my two dogs for their gracious appearance in this book.

ABOUT THE AUTHOR

SHIZUKA IJUIN aspired to be a professional baseball player before a shoulder injury thwarted his boyhood dream. After successful stints as an advertising
executive, a commercial director, and a pop song
writer, Ijuin became an acclaimed author. He met
Hideki Matsui after receiving the Naoki Prize for
Ukezuki (*The Moon of Accepting*), a collection of short
stories about baseball. Other honors include the
Yoshikawa Eiji Literary Award for new writers for
Chibusa (*The Breast*), the Shibata Renzaburo Award
for *Kikansha Sensei* (*Locomotive Teacher*), and the Yoshikawa Eiji Literary Award for *Goro Goro*. He lives in
Tokyo with his wife and two dogs.

ABOUT THE TYPE

This book was set in Garamond No. 3, a variation
of the classic Garamond typeface originally designed by the Parisian type cutter Claude Garamond
(1480–1561).

Claude Garamond's distinguished romans and
italics first appeared in *Opera Ciceronis* in 1543–44.
The Garamond types are clear, open, and elegant.